LeBron James

Basketball's King

By Ryan Nagelhout

Portions of this book originally appeared in
LeBron James by Anne Wallace Sharp.

LUCENT
P R E S S

Published in 2017 by
Lucent Press, an Imprint of Greenhaven Publishing, LLC
353 3rd Avenue
Suite 255
New York, NY 10010

Designer: Deanna Paternostro
Editor: Katie Kawa

Cataloging-in-Publication Data

Names: Nagelhout, Ryan.
Title: LeBron James: basketball's king / Ryan Nagelhout.
Description: New York : Lucent Press, 2017. | Series: People in the news |
Includes index.
Identifiers: ISBN 9781534560291 (library bound) | ISBN 9781534560307
(ebook)
Subjects: LCSH: James, LeBron--Juvenile literature. | Basketball players-
-United States--Biography--Juvenile literature.
Classification: LCC GV884.J36 N34 2017 | DDC 796.323092--dc23

Printed in the United States of America

CPSIA compliance information: Batch #CW17KL: For further information contact Greenhaven Publishing LLC,
New York, New York at 1-844-317-7404.

Please visit our website, www.greenhavenpublishing.com. For a free
color catalog of all our high-quality books, call toll free 1-844-317-7404
or fax 1-844-317-7405.

Contents

Foreword

We live in a world where the latest news is always available and where it seems we have unlimited access to the lives of the people in the news. Entire television networks are devoted to news about politics, sports, and entertainment. Social media has allowed people to have an unprecedented level of interaction with celebrities. We have more information at our fingertips than ever before. However, how much do we really know about the people we see on television news programs, social media feeds, and magazine covers?

Despite the constant stream of news, the full stories behind the lives of some of the world's most newsworthy men and women are often unknown. Who was Taylor Swift before she was a pop music phenomenon? What does LeBron James do when he is not playing basketball? What inspired Elon Musk to dream as big as he does?

This series aims to answer questions like these about some of the biggest names in pop culture, sports, politics, and technology. While the subjects of this series come from all walks of life and areas of expertise, they share a common magnetism that has made them all captivating figures in the public eye. They have shaped the world in some unique way, and—in many cases—they are poised to continue to shape the world for many years to come.

These biographies are not just a collection of basic facts. They tell compelling stories that show how each figure grew to become a powerful public personality. Each book aims to paint a complete, realistic picture of its subject—from the challenges they overcame to the controversies they caused. In doing so, each book reinforces the idea that even the most famous faces on the news are real people who are much more complex than we are often shown in brief video clips or sound bites. Readers are also reminded that there is even more to a person than what they present to the world through social media posts, press releases, and interviews. The whole story of a person's life can only be discovered by digging beneath the surface of their public persona, and that is what this series allows readers to do.

The books in this series are filled with enlightening quotes from speeches and interviews given by the subjects, as well as quotes and anecdotes from those who know their story best: family, friends, coaches, and colleagues. All quotes are noted to provide guidance for further research. Detailed lists of additional resources are also included, as are timelines, indexes, and unique photographs. These text features come together to enhance the reading experience and encourage readers to dive deeper into the stories of these influential men and women.

Fame can be fleeting, but the subjects featured in this series have real staying power. They have fundamentally impacted their respective fields and have achieved great success through hard work and true talent. They are men and women defined by their accomplishments, and they are often seen as role models for the next generation. They have left their mark on the world in a major way, and their stories are meant to inspire readers to leave their mark, too.

Introduction

From Prodigy to Pro

Prodigies—though remarkable—often are not remarkable for long. Immense talent surfacing at a young age is something to be celebrated, but the fame that comes with it is typically only temporary. In many cases, prodigies fear becoming ordinary. What happens if age ever catches up with the advanced abilities that once made someone stand out? Given enough time and a stalling of developing talent, a prodigy can simply turn into a regular person.

In sports, the term commonly used for someone with immense talent at a young age is not "prodigy" but "phenom." Short for "phenomenon," the phrase is best applied to those yet to play at a sport's highest level. It is the hockey player embarrassing smaller teammates in junior hockey or the running back in football blazing past overwhelmed defenders in the open field. Phenoms turn heads and raise expectations for a career that sometimes does not live up to the high hopes of those who are watching.

As an athlete's career develops, the word "phenom" is not used anymore. It is replaced by "star" or "superstar," if the athlete is good enough. However, much like a piano prodigy losing their way as they grow up or a chess prodigy growing bored with the game, turning phenoms into superstars is not always automatic. The hard work never stops.

LeBron James was a basketball prodigy who grew into a star in the National Basketball Association (NBA). His story is one of remarkable skill and dedication to a craft beyond anything those who have never been called a "phenom" could imagine. Entering the NBA as the last of the high school athletes allowed to skip college, his rise to the game's highest level signaled the closing of an era and the start of a new one: the dawn of King James's professional basketball career.

The Next Jordan or the First James?

James's career is unique in so many ways. Declared the heir apparent to one of basketball's most celebrated stars—Michael Jordan—James has been compared to Jordan for most of his life. How could anyone, critics asked, ever "be like Mike?" Few, if any, athletes have ever had such strong media attention at such an early age and for so long.

Sports fans around the world have an opinion on LeBron

Kids growing up today want to be the next LeBron James the same way kids growing up in the 1990s wanted to be the next Michael Jordan.

James, both as a person and a basketball player. The sheer amount of attention his life has received makes this possible. However, whether people love or hate him, it is now clear that James is one of the greatest to ever play professional basketball. Rising from poverty to become a young millionaire, he has won NBA titles in multiple cities with amazing performances on the court. He has changed the way the city of Cleveland looks at its sports teams by bringing a major sports championship to a city that had been without one for decades.

Over the course of his legendary career, critics always said that there would never be another Michael Jordan. They were right. This generation's basketball superstar is someone entirely new. He is Lebron James—the prodigy who went pro out of high school and changed the NBA forever.

Chapter One

The Young King James

LeBron Raymone James was born on December 30, 1984, in Akron, Ohio. He was born into a situation that is common for millions of children in America—a life of poverty. His mother, Gloria James, was a single mother who struggled to make ends meet. She was a 16-year-old high school student who lived at home with her mother, Freda, and her two brothers, Terry and Curt, when she discovered she was pregnant.

LeBron has always given his mother credit for being a stabilizing force in his life. Their strong relationship helped them endure the tragedies, challenges, and pitfalls they have faced on their very unique journey. LeBron has often called his mother the most significant influence on his life, and he even has her name tattooed on his arm. "My mother is my everything," LeBron has stated. "Always has been. Always will be."[1]

Although his mother is a constant presence in his life, LeBron's biological father has never been a part of his life. According to family sources, LeBron's father was an ex-convict who wanted no part in being a father or a family man. To this day, both LeBron and his mother refuse to speak about his biological father.

Hickory Street

LeBron and his mother spent his first few years of life living in his grandmother's home. Their house was located on Hickory Street in the middle of a poor neighborhood in Akron. Finances

LeBron's mother, Gloria James, has always been supportive of her son. Some opposing fans would even complain about her cheering at LeBron's games in high school!

were extremely tight for the entire James family. Most of the residents in the neighborhood earned minimum wage, and the James family was no exception. There was seldom enough money to pay the mortgage and other bills. With the unemployment rate particularly high in that section of Akron, the neighbors learned to work together and help each other. Although they were living in poverty, the James family still maintained a sense of stability thanks to Freda's influence and the community around them.

A Father Figure

When LeBron was eight months old, his mom began dating a man named Eddie Jackson. A few years older than Gloria, Eddie had excelled in sports in school but was, at the time, unemployed. He quickly became very attached to Gloria's son. LeBron grew to love Eddie, and even after he achieved basketball stardom, he considered him to be the most important father figure in his life. Years later, when LeBron began winning awards, he always thanked his mother Gloria and his "dad" Eddie for all the love and support they had provided.

While living with the James family, Eddie often spent his spare time playing with LeBron. He and the toddler spent hours playing games and wrestling on the floor. It was Eddie who helped Gloria set up a toy basketball set for LeBron's Christmas gift the year he turned three.

As the two of them were setting up the toy together on Christmas Eve, Eddie and Gloria heard a loud thump in the house and hurried to see what had happened. They found Freda James on the floor. She died shortly thereafter from a heart attack. Eddie and Gloria decided not to tell LeBron about his grandmother's death until after the holidays so he could enjoy Christmas morning and his new toy. LeBron was overjoyed with his present and played with it most of the day. He especially liked to dunk the ball while jumping as high as he could. Even as tragedy swirled around him, the toddler had discovered what would be the key to a better life for him and his family.

Moving to Elizabeth Park

After Freda's death, the situation for Gloria, Eddie, and LeBron deteriorated rapidly. Gloria was still only 19 years old, while her brother Terry was 22 and her brother Curt was only 12. Money was virtually nonexistent. Their neighbors on Hickory Street offered what they could, but there was no way Gloria could pay the mortgage on their broken-down home. As a result, the bank soon foreclosed on their mortgage, which means it took back the property because it was bought with borrowed money that was not being paid back, and turned the house over to the city of Akron. The house was eventually condemned by the city and destroyed.

The James family and Eddie were forced to move. Terry and Curt left to live together and fend for themselves, as did Eddie, while Gloria and LeBron were left to find their own housing, often depending on the kindness of neighbors and relatives.

Unable to stay permanently in any of their housing situations, Gloria was forced to find another place for herself and her small son to live. She and LeBron eventually moved to a housing project called Elizabeth Park, a complex that was old and long past its prime. The area consisted of hundreds of brick row houses with large areas of open space where the children could play.

It was also an area where drugs, alcohol, and crime were big problems. The Akron police made frequent visits to Elizabeth Park to help combat drive-by shootings and gang fights. It was a tough neighborhood for a boy to grow up in. As a young man, LeBron spoke about his childhood: "I've seen a lot of stuff that kids my age just don't see."[2]

Their years at Elizabeth Park were characterized by instability and desperation. Gloria and LeBron lived at Elizabeth Park off and on for more than six years, moving from one friend's home to another and never having a place to truly call their own. When LeBron was five years old, they moved a total of seven times in a year. "I just grabbed my little backpack, which held all the possessions I needed," LeBron once said about moving so many times as a child, "and said to myself what I always said to myself: It's time to roll."[3]

As was the case on Hickory Street, LeBron and his mother credit the help of community members for enabling them to survive.

Life with the Walkers

LeBron struggled to cope with his unstable situation, especially in school. During his fourth-grade year, he skipped many days of classes, preferring instead to stay home and play. Gloria did not know quite what to do, but a solution was found that gave LeBron some stability at a time when he desperately needed it. The solution came from Frankie Walker Sr., a man Gloria knew through some of LeBron's after-school activities, including football. Frankie and his wife, Pam, offered to take LeBron in and allow him to live with them until Gloria found a more settled living situation, and Gloria agreed.

Despite already having three children of their own, the Walkers opened their home to LeBron, who moved in with the family. For the next two years, LeBron lived with the Walkers during the week and then spent time with his mother on the weekends.

"It was like a new beginning for me," LeBron said. "When I moved in with the Walkers, I went from missing eighty-seven days my fourth-grade year to zero days in the fifth grade … I love them. They are like my family … I wouldn't be here without them."[4]

LeBron thrived in his new home environment. Up to that point, there had been nothing but chaos and confusion in his life because of the constant moving he and his mother had done. Now with the Walkers, there was consistency in his life. LeBron also learned about discipline and responsibility. Just like the Walker children, LeBron had certain chores he was expected to do around the house. The Walkers also gave him plenty of attention and affection. They always celebrated LeBron's birthday and had regular holiday celebrations that included LeBron and his mother.

Focusing on the Game

LeBron played football as a child and teenager, but he also continued to develop his love for basketball. It was Frankie Walker Sr. who encouraged LeBron to practice on the backboard and net installed in the Walkers' driveway. Walker coached organized basketball in a recreational league at the Summit Lake Community Center in Akron, which is an inner city center where boys and girls could learn to play various sports.

Walker began teaching LeBron how to play basketball and passed on his considerable knowledge of the game to the eager child. The coach discovered that LeBron, then a fourth-grader, was a natural and gifted young athlete. "I had never coached a kid who picked things up and excelled in them as quickly as LeBron," Walker said. "He began to approach the game of basketball the way a chess master approaches chess."[5]

LeBron was thrilled when he was invited to join Walker's recreational league. He spent hours on the practice court, shooting the basketball from every imaginable position. When LeBron entered the fifth grade, Walker was so impressed with LeBron's skills and knowledge of the game that he made the boy an assistant coach for the fourth-grade team. He told the other parents that LeBron, even at his young age, could already offer basketball insights to younger players because of his natural abilities. LeBron continues to pride himself on the knowledge and skills he developed during his early days playing basketball. "I'm an 'A' student in basketball," he has said. "We are all blessed with the gifts that God gave us and it's important to use your gifts the right way."[6]

AAU Ball

In his fifth-grade year, after playing in Walker's league, LeBron joined the Northeast Shooting Stars, a team that played in the Amateur Athletic Union (AAU). The AAU is one of the largest nonprofit sports organizations in the United States.

The Shooting Stars were coached by a man who would become another of LeBron's most important mentors, Dru Joyce II. Joyce was dedicated to the game of basketball and devoted his time to coaching youngsters throughout the Akron area. The coach's son Dru Joyce III (known as Little Dru) introduced LeBron to Sian Cotton and then to Willie McGee. Together, the four boys would later be nicknamed the "Fabulous (Fab) Four" by area basketball fans. They formed a friendship that lasted throughout their high school years and beyond. LeBron relied on this inner circle for support and love as things rapidly changed in his life.

King of the Irish

LeBron James entered high school with a solid foundation in basketball and with his home life relatively stable. He and his friends Joyce III, Cotton, and McGee chose to attend St. Vincent-St. Mary High School after they learned a popular area coach—Keith Dambrot—was hired to coach the basketball team. As they entered their freshman year at St. Vincent-St. Mary, the four boys set a goal for themselves—winning a state championship for the school.

LeBron played in a number of different basketball camps in high school, learning how to play and getting to know some of the best young players in the country.

St. Vincent-St. Mary High School—a small, inner city, Catholic school—was best known for its academics; more than 90 percent of its seniors went to college. Due to its serious academic standards, LeBron was forced to keep up his grades so he could play sports for the Fighting Irish.

One of LeBron's best friends in high school was Maverick Carter, who was a senior when LeBron was a freshman. Carter was a star basketball player and a good friend to LeBron—the two were so close that, despite not being related, they called each other "cousin." Surrounded by his friends, involved in both football and basketball, and challenged to improve his grades, LeBron thrived and matured during high school.

On the Gridiron

Although basketball was LeBron's best sport, he also excelled at football. He played on the St. Vincent-St. Mary's football team during his first three years of high school. In his freshman year, LeBron made an immediate impact on the team as a wide receiver. By the end of his first season of football, he had become one of the keys to the team's success on the field. In his junior year, LeBron helped lead the team to the Ohio state semifinals. He caught 62 passes that year while compiling more than 1,200 yards.

Gloria James attended all of LeBron's football games, fully supporting his decision to play. She did, however, fear LeBron would get injured playing the rough sport. Toward the end of LeBron's junior football season, Gloria's fears were realized when LeBron broke the index finger on his left hand in a playoff game. The injury did not keep him off the basketball court, but it did keep him from playing football again. James wanted to focus on basketball. He knew that was going to be his path to a career in professional sports.

Freshman on the Floor

Despite his skills in football, it was on the basketball court that LeBron truly excelled. Even as a freshman, LeBron was recognized as an up-and-coming star. "LeBron reminded me of an athletic Magic Johnson," Dambrot, his head coach, said. "He could rebound, pass, and defend … My feeling was that if he wanted to be the best ever, he had the talent to be, as long as he worked hard."[7]

Maverick Carter was the star player for the Irish at the time, but with James playing point guard, the team went undefeated and headed to the state championship. Thanks in part to LeBron's 25 points, St. Vincent-St. Mary beat Jamestown Greenview High School for the Ohio state title.

"LeBron is a basketball genius," Dambrot said after the game. "There is no other way to see it."[8]

No Sophomore Slump

LeBron grew another 3 inches (8 cm) the summer after his freshman year, making him 6 feet 7 inches (2.01 m) tall. After playing football in the fall, LeBron concentrated all his energy on basketball. A new player—Romeo Travis—made the "Fab Four" into the "Fabulous Five."

With LeBron leading the way, St. Vincent-St. Mary finished with a 27–1 record. The team's only blemish was a 1-point loss to Oak Hill Academy, Virginia, in a game where LeBron was severely hampered by back spasms.

LeBron quickly established himself as the best high school basketball player in the country thanks to his unique combination of size, speed, athleticism, and basketball IQ.

The St. Vincent-St. Mary Irish went on to win the Ohio Division III State Championship again that year. LeBron earned the tournament's Most Valuable Player (MVP) award and, in addition, was named first team All-State. He also became the first sophomore in Ohio's history to win the state's Mr. Basketball award, an honor given to the most outstanding high school player in the state. *USA Today* named him to its first team All-America high school team. By the end of the season, LeBron was ranked as one of the best high school basketball players in the country. Dambrot then announced that he was leaving St. Vincent-St. Mary to coach at the University of Akron, but LeBron had two more seasons left to play with the Irish.

"The Chosen One"

In LeBron's junior year, the small St. Vincent-St. Mary gym could no longer hold the large crowds that wanted to watch him play. The school decided to move most of its home games to the nearby and larger University of Akron's Rhodes Arena. Dru Joyce II had been hired as the new St. Vincent-St. Mary coach. With a challenging schedule against nationally ranked schools, James and the Irish had a tougher season. For the first time since LeBron had joined the Irish, the team lost two games in a row.

LeBron finished his junior year averaging 28 points and 9 rebounds per game, winning his second Mr. Basketball award. He was also named to the all-USA first team in both *USA Today* and *People* magazine, and he received the 2001–2002 Gatorade National Boys Basketball Player of the Year award. LeBron was clearly more talented than the other players around him, and people took notice. "It was like watching Serena Williams serve it up for the high school girls' tennis team," journalist Scott Fowler wrote. "James was strikingly better than everyone else on the court."[9]

The awards and the praise, however, were overshadowed by the Irish's loss in the Ohio state title game to Cincinnati's Roger Bacon High School by a score of 71–63. It was their first loss to an Ohio team since LeBron joined the team.

By the end of the state finals, LeBron had already received invitations to play for several college basketball teams. He expressed interest in playing for several schools, including the University of North Carolina, Duke University, the Ohio State University, the University of Michigan, and the University of Florida. However, it was unlikely he would ever play college basketball. James was destined for the pros.

On February 18, 2002, his picture appeared on the cover of *Sports Illustrated* magazine. Beside his photograph were the words "The Chosen One." The accompanying article was written by Grant Wahl. In it, NBA player and coach Danny Ainge said, "If I were a general manager, there are only four or five NBA players that I wouldn't trade to get him [LeBron] right now ... If LeBron came out this year, I wouldn't even have to think about it. I'd take him number one."[10]

After the *Sports Illustrated* article was released, LeBron attracted the attention of Cleveland Cavaliers coach John Lucas, who invited the high school student to practice with the team during the summer of 2002. Like other coaches before him, Lucas was amazed at LeBron's abilities and skills. However, this kind of contact with a high school player still in his junior year is not allowed by the NBA. As a result, Lucas was suspended for several games, and the Cavaliers were fined $150,000.

Not long after the Cavaliers workout, LeBron broke his wrist. During an AAU game, he had been undercut by another player while in the air and landed heavily on his non-shooting hand. It was a scary incident, but the star breathed a sigh of relief as he acknowledged that the fracture could have been much worse. A serious break, requiring surgery or long-term rehabilitation, could have jeopardized his future. As it was, LeBron was out of action for a good part of the summer. He still, however, attended a number of basketball camps around the country before his senior season.

Waiting to Go Pro

LeBron had grown to his present height of 6 feet 8 inches (2.032 m) tall by his senior year. Although LeBron had been approached by a number of colleges during his junior year, he had already made his decision: He would go directly to the NBA. Although no formal announcement had been made, the media had already guessed as much. Even before the basketball season began, the majority of sports writers were predicting that LeBron would be the top draft pick in that June's NBA draft.

LeBron was under a lot of pressure and dealt with a lot of media attention during his last year of high school. "Sometimes it got to be too much," he said. "Sometimes I would wake up and I didn't want to go to school at all because it drained me a lot."[11]

On National Television

Because of all the media attention, American sports fans had been reading about LeBron for more than a year, but most had never seen him play. That changed on December 12, 2002, when fans had the chance to see if what the media had been claiming was true. Sports network ESPN2 had announced that, for the first time, it would televise a high school basketball game. As fans

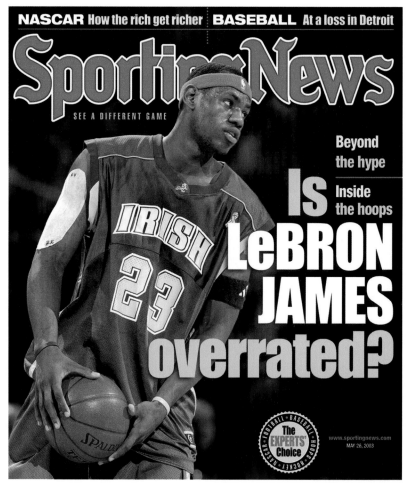

LeBron saw a lot of attention from the local and national media in his four years at St. Vincent-St. Mary High School, which overwhelmed him at times.

across the country tuned in that night, they were told that there was a sellout crowd at Cleveland State University Convocation Center to watch the much-publicized teenager play basketball. The game would give LeBron a chance to showcase his talents to sports fans across the country.

Broadcaster Dick Vitale and NBA star and Hall-of-Famer Bill Walton were on hand for the game. The broadcast was one of the top-rated shows in the network's history at that time.

St. Vincent-St. Mary took on rival Oak Hill Academy of Virginia that night in December. Oak Hill's team that year was led by all-star player Carmelo Anthony. The following year, Anthony would help Syracuse University win the National Collegiate Athletic Association (NCAA) men's basketball championship, and eventually, he would go on to become a star in the NBA. He and LeBron would also become good friends.

"I can't wait for the game," LeBron told reporters. "I'm going to put on a show."[12] LeBron was true to his word. He scored 31 points and had 13 rebounds and 6 assists in a 65–45 win. LeBron had proven that he was, indeed, worthy of all the praise that was being heaped on him.

Courting Controversy

Despite the big wins, controversy soon came for LeBron James. On January 10, 2003, the *Cleveland Plain Dealer* published a story about LeBron driving a brand-new Hummer SUV that had a DVD player, three televisions, a system for playing video games, and a leather interior. Questions immediately arose about how his family could afford such an expensive car. Rumors began to circulate that the car was a gift from one of the shoe companies that were interested in signing LeBron to an endorsement deal after he turned pro.

The Ohio High School Athletic Association (OHSAA) carried out an immediate investigation, led by Clair Muscaro. The question was whether the car purchase somehow violated the rules of amateur athletics that do not allow high school players to benefit financially or materially during their amateur careers. After a three-week investigation, however, the matter was dropped, and LeBron was cleared of all responsibility and blame.

LeBron's mother Gloria, it was discovered, had taken out a loan to buy the car based on LeBron's future potential earning power. Gloria admitted that the purchase was probably bad timing but that she and Eddie Jackson had investigated the matter thoroughly before buying the car. "We checked with everybody we needed before the vehicle was purchased," Eddie stated, "to make sure LeBron's eligibility wouldn't be jeopardized."[13]

Just days after the Hummer incident had been resolved, LeBron and his teammates traveled to Cleveland. While there, they went to Next Urban Gear, a popular store that sold jerseys and other sports items. While in the store, LeBron was approached by the store manager, Joe Hathorn, who gave LeBron two throwback jerseys valued at $845. The jerseys featured the names of Gale Sayers, of Chicago Bears football fame, and Wes Unseld, a well-known NBA player.

Not long after the store visit, OHSAA learned of the gifts and announced that LeBron would be suspended for violating their bylaws. LeBron James's high school career appeared to be over. Immediately after Muscaro's announcement, Gloria James contacted Cleveland lawyer Fred Nance to intervene on her son's behalf. When Nance investigated, he was told that the store owner gave LeBron the jerseys because of academic excellence, not athletic abilities. After much legal hassle, including an injunction against OHSAA that enabled LeBron to play, the matter was resolved to LeBron's benefit. The school ended up forfeiting one victory, while LeBron missed two games. He was then allowed to return to the basketball court.

A Successful Senior

Despite the scandals and the pressure from the media and elsewhere, LeBron finished the season playing some of his best basketball. During the last months of the basketball season, his team played some of the best teams in the country. The Irish went undefeated for the rest of the year and were called one of the best teams in Ohio high school history. They won their third state championship in four years, finishing the season with a 24–1 record.

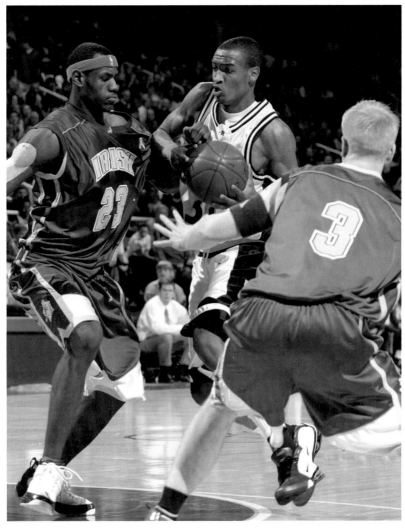

LeBron won three state championships while with the Irish and declared he would skip college and head right to the NBA after graduation. The NBA stopped drafting players straight out of high school not long after LeBron's draft year, making him one of the last players of his kind in the league.

Senior Night

As LeBron's senior year came to an end, St. Vincent-St. Mary held its annual Senior Night at the Irish's last home game. The night was used to acknowledge all the senior basketball players, along with their families. LeBron had been looking forward to the occasion as an opportunity to recognize his mother, along with Eddie Jackson, for everything they had done for him.

When the night arrived, however, both Gloria and Eddie were elsewhere. Eddie was in jail, convicted of mail and bank fraud. Gloria, on the other hand, was in court dealing with financial problems that had resulted from an accident LeBron had in his Hummer. She told LeBron that she would do her best to be there but could not guarantee she would make it.

With neither Gloria nor Eddie present, LeBron waited alone by the sidelines for his name to be announced. High school officials delayed the ceremony to give his mother ample time to appear, but at last, they had to proceed with the evening. His teammates and friends were announced first and walked proudly to center court with their parents. Then, it was LeBron's turn, and his name was called. As he walked forward, his friends left their parents and made their way toward LeBron. They encircled him with their arms and walked together to center court. LeBron then spoke to the crowd, saying: "Today was a special day for me and my teammates ... We grew up together, did a lot of things together."[1] What might have been a sad moment for LeBron instead became a moment that showed that his teammates were also his family.

1. Quoted in David Lee Morgan Jr., *LeBron James: The Rise of a Star.* Cleveland, OH: Gray & Company Publishers, 2003, p. 150.

LeBron was awarded his third straight Mr. Basketball award, which was something that no other player had ever achieved. It was also announced that one of LeBron's high school jerseys was going to the Naismith Memorial Basketball Hall of Fame, an unusual honor for a high school player.

After his high school season, James was invited to a number of All-Star games. Perhaps the biggest and best known of these games is the McDonald's High School All-American game, which is an event that has featured 15 top overall draft picks for the NBA. The 2003 McDonald's game was played at Gund Arena in Cleveland. The seats were filled with thousands of LeBron's fans. LeBron's team won 122–107, while LeBron himself made over 50 percent of his shots and won the John Wooden Award as the MVP. One NBA scout was overheard saying, "He's on a different level from these kids."[14]

Chapter Two

King of Cleveland

After graduating from high school, LeBron James was immediately projected to be the first pick in the NBA draft, meaning whoever won the NBA's draft lottery would get to pick James that summer. Sportswriter Michelle Kaufman discussed the common reasons people believed James would be chosen first:

Fans of many NBA teams were desperate for James to join their team, even making jerseys with his name on them before he was drafted.

Without question, LeBron is the best player in the draft, the kind of player who comes around once every fifteen years ... He is so versatile ... and he's not a good kid, he's a great kid. A marketing dream. He's the whole package and he'll be worth every penny someone pays for him.[15]

Nike, Reebok, and

James signed a lucrative contract with the shoe company Nike soon after leaving high school. He has had a successful business relationship with the company ever since then.

Adidas all wanted to sign James to a large shoe and athletic apparel contract. James chose Nike, signing a deal worth more than $90 million. It pales in comparison to the reported lifetime deal he signed with Nike in 2015, which is expected to be worth more than $1 billion. However, in 2003, after a long childhood in poverty, LeBron James was a multimillionaire, and this was before he ever played a single game of professional basketball.

First Overall

On May 22, 2003, LeBron James learned where he would play NBA basketball. The Cleveland Cavaliers had the best chance to win the league's draft lottery, but ping-pong balls would have to decide. All over Cleveland and northwest Ohio, people held their breath as they watched the televised lottery. Cheers erupted all over the area when Memphis was selected to take the second choice. That left Cleveland with the first pick—and LeBron James.

If any city was in need of a star player, it was Cleveland. The last time the city had won a championship in any major professional sport was in 1964, when the Cleveland Browns won the National Football League (NFL) Championship. Cleveland sports fans since then had struggled through losing season after losing season for all their major sports teams. The Cavaliers, or the Cavs, in particular had always been somewhat of a mockery. The team had lost 65 of 82 games in the 2002–2003 season. They needed a superstar to turn them around, and now they were getting one from nearby Akron. The Cavaliers finally made it official on June 6, 2003, when NBA Commissioner David Stern made the announcement that James had been selected by Cleveland. When interviewed after the announcement, James told reporters, "Ya'll come to Cleveland. It'll be lit up like Vegas."[16] He was clearly excited to be a Cavalier.

James was the first overall pick of the 2003 NBA draft.

Life in the Pros

James only faced more pressure to perform in the NBA. Although he tried to downplay expectations, many in Cleveland hoped he would be able to finally bring the city a championship. With media and fan interest high, James took the court for his first regular season pro game against the Sacramento Kings. At age 18, he was the youngest player on the floor. In the starting lineup, he played like a veteran. It was quickly obvious to the media and fans that he was the best Cavalier on the floor.

James won the NBA Rookie of the Year award in 2004.

Although the Cavaliers lost the game, James played well, scoring 25 points and adding 6 rebounds, 9 assists, and 4 steals. James's impact on the Cavs was immediate. Before James's signing, the team could barely give away tickets for their games. On opening night of their first home game that season, however, more than 20,000 fans saw James play.

James was also credited with turning around the Cavaliers' record that year. Largely as a result of James's play, the Cavaliers improved their record to 35–47. James averaged 20.9 points a game and was named NBA Rookie of the Year. He became the first Cavalier in franchise history and the youngest player in NBA history to earn this honor. He received 78 out of a possible 118 first-place votes.

James was one of the most popular players in the NBA during his rookie year. He was always a crowd favorite and never failed to sign autographs for children after the games.

Toward the end of his rookie year, James was selected to represent the United States as a member of the 2004 men's Olympic basketball team. At age 19, he was the youngest player on the team, and he was the first Cavalier ever to play on an Olympic team. "It's a dream come true for me to represent my country,"[17] James said of the honor. Despite his skills, however, he saw little action in Olympic competition. The team won the bronze medal game, finishing in third.

Sophomore Season

LeBron James made the Cleveland Cavaliers relevant again in his rookie season. In his second year as a pro, he made them competitive. During his sophomore season (2004–2005), James led the Cavaliers to their first season with a winning record in seven years. During that time, he played more minutes per game than anyone else in the league, and he also ranked third in scoring, averaging 27.2 points per game. James was also third in steals and sixth in assists, averaging 7.2 assists per game. He became the youngest player in NBA history to score 50 points in a game and to record a triple-double (achieving double-digit figures in three

Business Off the Court

When James entered the NBA, he hired an agent, Aaron Goodwin, to represent him in all contract negotiations both on and off the court. In 2005, however, James fired Goodwin. Shortly thereafter, he announced that he was forming his own management company. While he would be the president of the company, it would be run by his friends Maverick Carter, Randy Mims, and Rich Paul. Mims is James's uncle, and the other two are good friends from his high school years. The group has helped James negotiate a number of endorsement deals with companies around the world.

James said very early in his career that he wanted to become a billionaire through smart business decisions:

In the next 15 or 20 years, I hope I'll be the richest man in the world. That's one of my goals. I want to be a billionaire. I want to get to a position where generation on generation don't have to worry about [anything]. I don't want family members from my kids to my son's kids to ... have to worry. And I can't do that now just playing basketball.[1]

James worked hard as both a basketball player and a businessman to become successful and financially stable. Thanks to his basketball talent and his business deals, he has secured a better life for his family than the life he had as a child.

1. Quoted in Associated Press, "AP Interview: LeBron James _ Beyond his Years, Beyond the Hype," ESPN.com, December 10, 2005. www.espn.com/espn/wire/_/section/nba/id/2254792.

offensive categories such as scoring, rebounding, and assists).

Coach Paul Silas was among the many who praised James's game: "I have never seen a player learn so much in one year. He is further ahead than I thought he would be at this time."[18]

During his second season with the Cavaliers, James became one of the NBA's most athletic players and earned glowing praise as the undisputed Cavalier team leader.

James was voted to the NBA All-Star team that year. He enjoyed playing with the best players in professional basketball—a budding superstar among other superstars. He played well, scoring 13 points, 8 assists, and 6 rebounds. At the time, James was only the second Cavs player in team history to make the game.

James and the Cavs finished with a record of 42–40 during his second season in the NBA, but they failed to make the playoffs once again. However, as Howard Beck wrote in the *New York Times*, "If the Cavaliers fail, it will not be for lack of effort by James."[19] He did everything he could to help his team win.

Making the Postseason

During James's third season with the Cavaliers (2005–2006), the team had a 50–32 record and made the playoffs for the first time in 8 years. James was outstanding, averaging 31.4 points per game and finishing second in NBA MVP voting behind Phoenix's Steve Nash. He also made his second NBA All-Star Game, scoring 29 points in a win and also taking home the game's MVP award.

In James's playoff debut against the Washington Wizards, he had 32 points, 11 rebounds, and 11 assists and became only the third player in NBA history to have a triple-double in a first playoff appearance. He fell just short of another triple-double in his second playoff game, and for the entire series, he averaged 35.7 points, shooting 50 percent from the field as the Cavs beat the Wizards in six games.

Next, the Cavaliers faced the Detroit Pistons, the top-seeded team in the Eastern Conference. Cleveland actually led the series after five games, but the Cavs failed to close Detroit out, losing in seven games.

First Finals

The next three seasons proved to be fruitful and challenging for LeBron James and the Cavaliers. Cleveland finished with their second straight 50–32 record in the 2006–2007 season. James averaged 27.3 points per game and scored twice as many points as the next Cavs player.

Cleveland made the playoffs for the second straight year, once again taking on the Washington Wizards in the first round of the postseason. Cleveland swept the Wizards in four games,

A Helping Hand

As both an NBA superstar and an Olympian, James has made consistently positive contributions to his teams on the basketball court. He has also made a tremendous impact on the black communities of Cleveland and Akron. According to James, since high school, he has wanted to help others who were growing up in similar circumstances to his own. For this reason, he and his family formed the LeBron James Family Foundation.

The foundation has been successful in raising large sums of money for the underprivileged. They do so, in part, by sponsoring a number of events and giveaways. In addition to James's philanthropic work in northeast Ohio, he has also been very active elsewhere. James personally donated more than $200,000 worth of supplies to Hurricane Katrina victims. He has worked closely with Boys Hope Girls Hope, an organization that helps place children facing serious family problems and poverty in temporary but more stable living situations. James is particularly interested in this program because of his own experience living with the Walkers.

To recognize James's efforts in the community, the

then the team took care of the New Jersey Nets to reach the Eastern Conference Finals. The Cavs lost the first two games of the series in Detroit, then they led a furious comeback to win the next four games.

In the series' defining moment, the Cavs won a dramatic Game 5 in double overtime. James scored 29 of Cleveland's last 30 points, including the game-winning layup with two seconds left on the clock in the game's second overtime. James finished with 48 points, 9 rebounds, and 7 assists. Marv Albert, who was one of the announcers for the game, called it "one of the greatest

NBA awarded him with the Community Assist Award in June 2006.

James has been involved in many charitable efforts and community outreach programs during his career.

In 2006, James and the Cavs swept the Washington Wizards in four games, but they were later swept by the San Antonio Spurs in the NBA Finals.

moments in postseason history."[20] Cleveland won the series in six games to win their first Eastern Conference Championship and make the NBA Finals.

In Cleveland's first NBA Finals appearance, they faced a veteran team in the San Antonio Spurs. James and the Cavs looked young and overpowered by established superstar Tim Duncan and the Spurs, who swept all four games to win the NBA Championship. Cleveland lost Game 3 at home by only 3 points and Game 4 by just 1, but the results were clear: James and the Cavs still needed to grow up a bit before they could truly contend for an NBA title.

James and the Cavs made the playoffs for a third straight season in 2007–2008. He also made another NBA All-Star team, winning his second All-Star MVP award in a victory for the East. James became Cleveland's all-time leading scorer in a March 21, 2008, game against the Toronto Raptors, passing Brad Daugherty on the list. Cleveland went 45–37 that season, but in the postseason, James and the Cavs struggled. Cleveland beat Washington in the first round for the second straight season but met a tough matchup against the Boston Celtics. In a tight seven-game series, Cleveland won all three home games but couldn't keep up with Boston's Big Three—Paul Pierce, Kevin Garnett, and Ray Allen—along with rookie standout Rajon Rondo. James had 45 points in the decisive Game 7, but Paul Pierce scored 41 to lift Boston to a 97–92 win on its home court.

With a trip to the playoffs now the norm in Cleveland, the 2008–2009 season became a test both personally for James and for the Cavaliers as a team. James was brilliant again, averaging 28.4 points per game. Though his career-high 30-point average came a year earlier, James was named the NBA MVP at age 24. He led Cleveland into the postseason as the top seed in the Eastern Conference after a 66–16 record in the regular season. Cleveland cruised through the first two rounds of the playoffs, sweeping Detroit in the opening round and Atlanta in the Eastern Conference Semifinals.

The Eastern Conference Finals featured a showdown between James's Cavs and Dwight Howard's Orlando Magic. Despite 49 points from James in Game 1 of the series, Orlando won, 107–106. The Cavs bounced back to win Game 2, but they lost the next 3 games to get knocked out of the postseason in 5 games. James had many amazing individual performances throughout Cleveland's four straight playoff appearances, but they were unable to put together great team efforts against the best teams in the league when it really counted. James was starting to think he would need some help to win an NBA title.

Chapter **Three**

The Decision

In the summer of 2010, LeBron James made a decision that changed the way millions viewed him and his basketball career. For the first time since he decided to skip college and join the NBA, James could decide for himself where he wanted to play. He was about to enter free agency. After seven years in Cleveland, James was allowed to decide which team he joined for the 2010–2011 NBA season.

The process was on the minds of NBA fans and executives for weeks. James met with six teams—the Cavaliers, Chicago Bulls, Los Angeles Clippers, Miami Heat, New Jersey Nets, and New York Knicks—in a downtown Cleveland office building. Fans of each team wanted James—the league's best player—to choose their team and help them win an NBA title. Fans of other teams were mad their team was never even given a chance to talk to James. Team owners, general managers, coaches, and players took part in elaborate presentations to James, while journalists waited outside the office building to report on the meetings each day. Everyone speculated about where James would end up. His decision would impact the league's other players as well: Many players did not sign with teams on July 1, the date when free agency begins in the NBA, because no one knew where James would end up playing.

Playoff Shortcomings

One major reason James even considered going to a new team in free agency was his frustration with his inability to win an NBA title in Cleveland. With James in Cleveland, the Cavs had never been better. They made the NBA Finals for the first time in team history and made the postseason in five straight seasons. However, a lack of talent—most notably a lack of depth throughout the rest of the roster—made those playoff experiences tough lessons for James and the Cavs. They were overmatched against the Spurs in their trip to the Finals in 2007 and struggled to match the veteran presence and young depth of the Boston Celtics in 2008 and again in 2010, when the Cavs lost in the Eastern Conference Semifinals.

James was visibly frustrated after losses many times, and he received harsh criticism from the media in 2009 when he walked off the court before shaking hands with Orlando Magic players after they knocked off the Cavs in Game 6 of the Eastern Conference Finals. James also skipped a postgame session with the media, which angered NBA writers around the country.

During the summer of 2009, James was asked about the "black eye" he had with the media for his behavior after losing to the Magic. He defended his decision to not shake hands but apologized for missing his time with the media. He told reporters,

I still haven't had a black eye, for one. Two, I don't regret anything that I do. The only thing I apologize for that night is not doing the media [session, after the game].

The media, your ... job don't start until ours' finish. You guys can't report and write you guys' story until we take a shower, until we come out and sit on the podium. That's the only thing I

apologize for. As far as shaking hands, it's something that is not done in the NBA. If it was something like tennis, after tennis, you play, you win, you lose, you go to the center and shake hands, it happens every game in tennis.

James pointed out that, unlike in some other sports such as tennis and hockey, shaking hands with the other team's players is not a well-known tradition in the NBA. "I'm not a poor sport at all," he continued. "You can ask anyone that knows me."[21]

James repeated that his goal was to win a title with Cleveland, and anything less than that was unacceptable. "My expectations are us competing for a championship," he said. "That's the only expectation I have going into the season. I'm at a point in my career, if I'm not competing for an NBA championship, it's a failure, as a full season."[22]

James made it quite clear that he was tired of failing. However, the Cavs also came up short in the race for a championship in 2010, failing once again by James's standards. Many thought he would leave Cleveland for a better shot at winning a title. Many more, however, thought he would not leave his hometown team for greener pastures.

"Taking My Talents to ..."

On July 7, the world learned not where LeBron James would play, but how everyone would find out—on the television channel ESPN. It was announced that his choice of destination would be revealed in a 75-minute ESPN special called *The Decision*. After years of speculation about where James would sign in one of the most anticipated free agency periods in modern sports history, fans finally knew it was about to come to an end.

On July 8, in a live broadcast shot at a Boys and Girls Club in Greenwich, Connecticut, James was interviewed by sportscaster Jim Gray. About 30 minutes into the show, James finally told the world where he was signing:

James received a lot of criticism for the airing of his *Decision* special, especially because he chose not to return to the Cleveland Cavaliers.

> *Gray: The answer to the question everyone wants to know: LeBron, what's your decision?*

> *James: In this fall ... this is very tough ... in this fall I'm going to take my talents to South Beach and join the Miami Heat ... I feel like it's going to give me the best opportunity to win and to win for multiple years, and not only just to win in the regular season or just to win five games in a row or three games in a row, I want to be able to win championships. And I feel like I can compete down there.[23]*

It was a moment that changed the basketball world forever. James was leaving Cleveland for Miami. In the process, he joined superstar Dwyane Wade and new Heat forward Chris Bosh, who had signed with the Heat days earlier. Not even the teams James met with knew about his decision until moments before he announced it live on air. Cleveland fans were stunned. Heat fans were thrilled. People who were not fans of the six teams courting James sympathized with Cavaliers fans for losing their hero to a larger market that had already won an NBA title in 2006.

Many were shocked that James would make such a large spectacle of his leaving Cleveland. Most did not understand how the program got so much airtime on ESPN or who was making money from the ads sold for the event. The truth is that Jim Gray pitched the idea for *The Decision* to James. Gray, Maverick Carter, and ESPN vice president John Skipper worked with James to create the program. ESPN donated the broadcast time to James, and the money from the ads sold—more than $6 million—was to be donated to charity. The Boys and Girls Club received $2.5 million from the event, which was ESPN's highest rated non-NFL broadcast of the year.

Plenty of sportswriters around the country criticized James for the way he acted in free agency and for taking part in *The Decision*. "You can't spell James without 'me,' and it's more difficult to defend James for this arrogant exercise than it is to defend him in the pick and roll,"[24] wrote Ethan Skolnick of the *South Florida Sun-Sentinel*.

Mitch Albom of the *Detroit Free Press* had one of the hotter takes on James's Decision. He thought the move was self-indulgent and that the event's charitable purpose did not make up for the spectacle it caused:

You want to give to charity, quietly write a check. Don't get a network to do it for you so it gets to pump its shows and you get to shower yourself in international coverage—while calling it philanthropy. The NBA has embarrassed itself here. The media have embarrassed themselves. And a guy who calls himself 'King' may be beyond embarrassment, which is truly embarrassing.[25]

Others were worried how this would impact James's "brand" and many of his endorsements. "James isn't an athlete," wrote Paul Daugherty of the *Cincinnati Enquirer*. "That's too confining. He is a 'brand.' So while some of us shake our heads at the nonsense of turning a career decision into a prime-time TV production, others of us marvel at the way LeBron is playing the game. And we're not talking basketball."[26]

Cleveland Responds

Thousands of fans in Cleveland were heartbroken that LeBron James left the Cavaliers. Some took to the streets to burn his jersey. Many swore they would never root for him again.

A larger-than-life mural of James on the side of Cleveland's arena was taken down after he chose to play in Miami.

Gilbert's Letter

Below is the text of Cleveland owner Dan Gilbert's letter to Cavs fans after James's decision to leave Cleveland for Miami:

Dear Cleveland, All Of Northeast Ohio and Cleveland Cavaliers Supporters Wherever You May Be Tonight;

As you now know, our former hero, who grew up in the very region that he deserted this evening, is no longer a Cleveland Cavalier.

This was announced with a several day, narcissistic, self-promotional build-up culminating with a national TV special of his "decision" unlike anything ever "witnessed" in the history of sports and probably the history of entertainment.

Clearly, this is bitterly disappointing to all of us.

The good news is that the ownership team and the rest of the hard-working, loyal, and driven staff over here at your hometown Cavaliers have not betrayed you nor NEVER will betray you.

There is so much more to tell you about the events of the recent past and our more than exciting future. Over the next several days and weeks, we will be communicating much of that to you.

You simply don't deserve this kind of cowardly betrayal.

You have given so much and deserve so much more.

In the meantime, I want to make one statement to you tonight:

"I PERSONALLY GUARANTEE THAT THE CLEVELAND CAVALIERS WILL WIN AN NBA CHAMPIONSHIP BEFORE THE SELF-TITLED FORMER 'KING' WINS ONE"

You can take it to the bank.

If you thought we were motivated before tonight to bring the hardware to Cleveland, I can tell you that this shameful display of selfishness and betrayal by one of our very own has shifted our "motivation" to previously unknown and previously never experienced levels.

Some people think they should go to heaven but NOT have to die to get there.

Sorry, but that's simply not how it works.

This shocking act of disloyalty from our home grown "chosen one" sends the exact opposite lesson of what we would want our children to learn. And "who" we would want them to grow-up to become.

But the good news is that this heartless and callous action can only serve as the antidote to the so-called "curse" on Cleveland, Ohio.

The self-declared former "King" will be taking the "curse" with him down south. And until he does "right" by Cleveland and Ohio, James (and the town where he plays) will unfortunately own this dreaded spell and bad karma.

Just watch.

Sleep well, Cleveland.

Tomorrow is a new and much brighter day....

I PROMISE you that our energy, focus, capital, knowledge and experience will be directed at one thing and one thing only:

DELIVERING YOU the championship you have long deserved and is long overdue....

Dan Gilbert
Majority Owner
Cleveland Cavaliers[1]

1. Quoted in "Letter from Cavs Owner Dan Gilbert," ESPN.com, December 13, 2010. www.espn.com/nba/news/story?id=5365704.

Others were simply shocked that James would leave them. News crews interviewed fans who said things such as "He's dead to me"[27] on camera.

Cavaliers owner Dan Gilbert reacted publicly as well, publishing an open letter to Cavs fans that attacked James for leaving Cleveland behind. The letter, published on the team's official website and quickly spread around the Internet, was written in the childish typeface Comic Sans. Gilbert called James a "coward" and called *The Decision* a "shameful display of selfishness and betrayal by one of our very own." The letter also included a sentence in all capital letters in which the owner promised the city of Cleveland that the Cavs would win an NBA title "BEFORE THE SELF-TITLED FORMER 'KING' WINS ONE."[28]

Many thought the letter was an overreaction on Gilbert's part and perhaps a little immature. However, plenty of fans in Cleveland truly did feel betrayed by James. Without James, the Cavaliers were sure to struggle. Despite Gilbert's claims that "brighter" days would come for the Cavs, they were much worse without James on the team. They immediately became one of the worst teams in the NBA and missed the playoffs for the next four seasons.

A Sign-and-Trade

Despite the fact that it took less than 75 minutes for James to announce his decision to join the Heat, the actual paperwork involved in signing with the team was a bit more complicated. James actually signed a six-year, $110 million deal with Cleveland—not Miami—on July 9, 2010.

The move—called a sign-and-trade—helped both teams in very different ways. Cleveland was given draft picks and options to make their team better to try to lessen the impact of losing the league's best player. Miami, on the other hand, was given more flexibility with its contracts. By not signing James to a contract directly, Miami did not have to offer him a more expensive contract that the team could not fit under its salary cap, or the amount of money it is allowed to spend

James joined Dwyane Wade and free agent Chris Bosh
in Miami.

on players. James made $14.5 million in his first season with
the Heat, which was the same amount as Chris Bosh, who was
also signed-and-traded to Miami by the Toronto Raptors. This
allowed Miami to fill out the rest of its roster with players and
create a more balanced team.

"I have not had a full max deal yet in my career—that's a story
untold," James told ESPN in 2013. "I don't get (the credit) for it.
That doesn't matter to me; playing the game is what matters to
me. Financially, I'll sacrifice for the team. It shows for some of
the top guys, it isn't all about money. That's the genuine side of
this, it's about winning. I understand that."[29]

In return for James, Cleveland received two second-round draft
picks and two first-round draft picks from the Heat to be used
in future NBA drafts. "This deal provides us with multiple key
assets and additional flexibility as we move forward for both the

short term and beyond,"[30] Cavaliers general manager Chris Grant said at the time.

Miami initially contacted Cleveland about a potential sign-and-trade the morning of July 9, offering only a second-round pick in the 2012 draft. Grant took Heat president Pat Riley's offer to Cavs owner Dan Gilbert—who hours earlier had written his infamous open letter to the city of Cleveland. According to a story by ESPN's Brian Windhorst, the two teams played a "high-stakes game of chicken" in getting the sign-and-trade done:

> Grant knew they had to do it. Fueled by some mix of anger and desperation, the Cavs countered: two first-round picks, two second-round picks and the option to swap picks with Miami in the 2012 draft.
>
> It would be an unprecedented haul for an unprecedented player, a ridiculous counteroffer to make for a guy who already said he belonged to Miami. It was also a shrewd move.
>
> Turns out, the Heat had a pressing self-imposed deadline: The team was throwing a party for its new Big Three later that night. It was a sold-out rock concert, complete with dry ice, hydraulic lifts and a light show.[31]

The Cavs also had the option of swapping first round picks with Miami in the 2012 draft, but that would not happen. Chris Bosh was also acquired on a sign-and-trade, which sent Heat draft picks to Toronto. Because of the sign-and-trades, the Heat made one pick in both the 2011 and 2012 NBA drafts. However, in the summer of 2010, that did not matter—Miami had a party to throw.

Miami threw a massive party for James, Wade, and Bosh after *The Decision*.

Welcome to Miami

One day after *The Decision* aired and hours after Miami and Cleveland completed the sign-and-trade, James was officially introduced to Miami fans at a party-like press conference. James was given a lavish welcome along with new signee Chris Bosh, and Heat veteran Dwyane Wade also made an appearance. Bosh, James, and Wade came out to pyrotechnic displays and a cheering crowd, with the words "YES. WE. DID." on video boards behind them.

All three players spoke to the crowd. Wade, who had been playing for Miami since he was drafted in 2003, was thrilled James and Bosh were joining him on the Heat. "You always want to put yourself in the best position possible to be able to win," Wade said, "and having an opportunity to be able to team up with arguably the best trio to ever play the game of basketball, it's amazing."[32]

When James was asked how it felt to be wearing a Heat

LeBron in Vegas

A few weeks after James made his decision live on air, ESPN published a story written by ESPN Los Angeles writer Arash Markazi. The piece was a narrative about James hosting a three-day party at a Las Vegas casino. In the piece, James and his friends—including Maverick Carter, a Nike executive, and fellow NBA player Chris Paul—are described as bouncing between nightclubs and casinos. Markazi described the events in detail, including a dance-off between James and NBA player Lamar Odom:

The more you hang around James, the more you realize he's still a child wrapped in a 6-foot-8, 250-pound frame. The night after the party at Tao, he and his crew walk through the casino at the Wynn and Encore and he pretends to dribble a basketball as he walks past ringing slot machines and tourists who do double-takes. In a Nike T-shirt, jeans and sneakers ... He stops every few feet to shoot a jump shot, his right hand extended above his head on the follow through. He weaves through a pack of a dozen friends and pretends to connect on a layup as he walks past a gift shop. He passes overhead casino signs and jumps up and slaps them, pretending to dunk. Columns covered with advertisements for lounge acts become stationary defenders, chumps to fake out before connecting on imaginary mid-range jump shots.

James probably goes through a practice's worth of shots as we walk from the XS nightclub at Encore (James left his poolside table when he saw the club was practically empty), through Wynn and over the bridge to the Palazzo.

uniform, he replied, "It feels right to be in this position, to wear this Heat uniform."[33]

James was vocal about his championship hopes as a part of

Soon after arriving at Lavo, a restaurant and nightclub at the Palazzo, a scene straight out of "West Side Story" breaks out when James and Lamar Odom, seated at a nearby table, engage in an impromptu dance-off to California Swag District's "Teach Me How to Dougie."[1]

The story, which appeared online on July 28, 2010, was soon pulled off the website. Though many speculated that James and his representatives pressured ESPN to pull the piece off its website, ESPN denied any outside influence in their decision. Instead, they blamed their reporter for not properly identifying himself to James. ESPN also claimed that the story was accidentally put on a server and published on the website without proper editing.

Markazi said that "it is important to note that I stand by the accuracy of the story in its entirety, but should have been clearer in representing my intent to write about the events I observed."[2]

The sports website Deadspin saved screenshots of the story and republished it online. While some might see it as a narrative about a successful 25-year-old basketball player having fun with his friends, others were more critical. They questioned James's maturity and willingness to celebrate while so many fans in Cleveland were heartbroken by his decision to join the Heat.

1. Quoted in Tommy Craggs, "Read ESPN's Spiked Story About LeBron Among the Naked Ladies in Vegas," Deadspin, July 28, 2010. deadspin.com/5598719/read-espns-spiked-story-about-lebron-among-the-naked-ladies-in-vegas.

2. Quoted in Ronald Blum, "ESPN.com Removes Article on James in Las Vegas," *The Seattle Times*, July 29, 2010. www.seattletimes.com/sports/espncom-removes-article-on-james-in-las-vegas/.

a new team of superstars. When asked about how many NBA titles he hoped to win in Miami, James assured the crowd that he came to Miami to think big: "Not two, not three, not four,

LeBron James quickly endeared himself to fans in Miami upon his arrival, promising multiple NBA title wins.

not five, not six, not seven …"[34] James said, trailing off as the American Airlines Arena crowd roared.

"In that moment on July 9, amid the pyrotechnics, the Miami Heat became a national Rorschach test," wrote journalist Howard Beck in the *New York Times*. "Everyone saw something: greatness, arrogance, self-indulgence, boldness, cowardice, pride, friendship, collusion, joy, cynicism, heroes, mercenaries."[35] It was hard to find a sports fan, especially a basketball fan, who did not have an opinion about LeBron James and his new teammates in the summer of 2010.

Changing Perceptions

The summer of 2010 changed the way many people perceived LeBron James. People in Cleveland thought he was a traitor. Those who watched him play in the last few postseason runs thought he might even be a quitter. Some thought he was just seeking attention and did not know how to be a normal 25-year-old. However, no matter what people thought about

James brought his pregame ritual—tossing powdered chalk up in the air—to Miami when he joined the Heat.

James and his decision to leave Cleveland, one thing was clear: He needed to win an NBA title. It was time for King James to finally take the crown.

Chapter Four

Winning in Miami

After an eventful, life-changing summer of 2010, LeBron James got back to basketball. His time in Miami, however, did not get off to a stellar start. His first game with the Heat came on October 26, 2010. James scored 31 points in an 88–80 loss to the Boston Celtics, the same team that eliminated James and the Cavs from the postseason earlier that year. Three nights later, the Heat did win their home opener, 96–70, against the Orlando Magic and proceeded to win their next three games as well. Miami did struggle, however, and started the season 9-8, hovering around the .500 mark—an equal number of wins and losses—until the end of November.

On December 2, LeBron James and the Miami Heat went to Cleveland to play the Cavaliers. James scored a season-high 38 points and had 5 rebounds and 8 assists in a 118–90 Heat win over James's former team. The Quicken Loans Arena crowd booed James every time he touched the ball, but the Heat cruised to the win as Cleveland suffered its worst loss of the season. James scored 24 points in the third quarter of that game—a Miami Heat record.

From there, the Heat took off. James's return to Cleveland was the Heat's third straight win, and they cruised to nine more victories after that to rise in the Eastern Conference standings. In fact, between November 29 and January 9 of that season, Miami lost just once—a 98–96 Dallas Mavericks win in Miami on December 20. Overall, the Heat won a franchise record

Fans in Cleveland booed James when he returned with the Heat, though tempers cooled as seasons went on.

15 games in December. They also set the NBA record for most road wins in a month, with 10 victories away from Miami.

James, Wade, and Bosh all made the NBA All-Star Game that season, which was the first time in franchise history that three Heat players made the game's roster. James led the East in minutes and scored 29 points in the 148–143 West win. Throughout the 2011 season, James led Miami with 26.7 points per game. James also averaged 7.5 rebounds and 7 assists per game. He finished third in league MVP voting behind Chicago's Derrick Rose and Orlando's Dwight Howard. James had a successful first regular season in Miami, but the real test was still to come. Could he lead his new team to the championship he left Cleveland to win?

The First Test

Miami finished the season with a 58–24 record, which was good for first place in the Southeast Division and the second seed in the Eastern Conference. The Heat averaged 102.1 points per game, the most in the conference, but also saw teams score

94.6 points per game against them. Their first-round playoff series was against the Philadelphia 76ers. The Heat took care of Philadelphia in five games, moving on to the next round.

The Heat played the Boston Celtics next, but James's rivals were also knocked out in five games by Miami. The Heat took the first 2 games of the series at home, while Boston only won Game 3. James averaged 28 points per game in the series.

Miami then faced the Chicago Bulls in the Eastern Conference Finals. After a blowout loss in the first game in Chicago, the Heat took over to win 4 straight games for another 4–1 series win. James averaged 25.8 points per game and helped Miami in a wild Game 5 win where they trailed 77–65 with 3:14 left and still came back to win. James had 8 points in the frantic comeback, including a 3-point shot that tied the game at 79 with a minute left and a jump shot that gave Miami the lead. He also blocked a shot in the game's dying seconds. The Eastern Conference championship for Miami meant that James would appear in his third straight NBA Finals.

This time, James and the Heat were matched up against the Western Conference champion Dallas Mavericks. Dallas reached the Finals after series wins over the Portland Trail Blazers, a sweep of the Los Angeles Lakers, and a Conference Finals win over the Oklahoma City Thunder. Led by Dirk Nowitzki, Dallas had actually met the Heat in the Finals in 2006, which was a series Dwyane Wade and Miami won in six games.

This time, however, Dallas was ready for Miami's "Big Three." Miami did take Game 1, with a 92–84, at home, but the Heat blew a fourth-quarter lead in Game 2 to lose by a score of 95–93. Miami bounced back in Game 3, winning 88–86 on a basket from Chris Bosh. From there, however, Dallas won 3 straight games and clinched the title with a 105–95 win in Game 6 in Miami.

James struggled in the series, and he finished behind Wade and Bosh in scoring, averaging just 17.8 points per game. In Game 4, which Miami lost 86–83, James had just 8 points. Many critics put a lot of pressure on James for his performance in the NBA Finals, and some speculated that the star could not show up for his team when it mattered most. "LeBron James was a flop in

James faced plenty of criticism from fans and the media when the Heat fell short of an NBA title in his first season in Miami.

the NBA Finals,"[36] wrote reporter Charles Hollis. Nowitzki was named the NBA Finals MVP after averaging 26 points, 9.7 rebounds, and 2 assists.

James's first season in Miami was a success in many ways. It proved that the "Big Three" of James, Wade, and Bosh could play well together, and they immediately made Miami one of the best teams in the league. However, their postseason failure continued the narrative established by many of James' critics: "King James" could not win when it mattered most. After a year when many in Cleveland and around the basketball world hoped that James would fail, he did, but he would soon prove he was more motivated than ever.

Locked Out

James's second season in Miami would have to wait. The labor agreement between NBA owners and its players expired during the summer of 2011, and, with no new contract set, the next NBA season did not start on time. Instead, the league entered into a period known in sports as a lockout. While the NBA Players Association and team owners negotiated a new deal, James and the rest of the NBA players tried to stay in shape. James worked out with NBA legend Hakeem Olajuwon during this time, trying to improve his game after a third straight season that ended in defeat in the NBA Finals. He also played in an exhibition game in Baltimore over the summer that featured fellow NBA stars Kevin Durant, Chris Paul, and Carmelo Anthony. Ticket sales from the event were donated to charitable causes close to Anthony's heart.

Negotiations between the league and the players association took months, and often it appeared that—like the National Hockey League in 2004–2005—a season might not happen. However, on November 26, 2011, the lockout came to a tentative end. The late-November deal allowed the 2011–2012 season to happen. On Christmas Day, the NBA began a 66-game schedule. James and the Heat could make another run at an NBA title. He and many other NBA players were ready to get back to basketball.

Four Straight Finals

James and the Heat were ready to take on the rest of the league once the season finally got underway. Miami started by getting revenge on the Dallas Mavericks, beating them in Dallas on Christmas Day, with a 105–94 win as the Mavericks celebrated their championship win against the Heat. Miami started the 2011–2012 season with five straight wins, with their only loss in their first nine games going to the Atlanta Hawks in early January. Miami cruised through the 66-game schedule, winning 46 games and finishing first in the Southeast Division for a second straight season. James and Wade started for the East team in the NBA All-Star Game, while Bosh was a reserve player.

Even in the short season, James was dominant and continued to break records. On January 16 in a game against Milwaukee, he became the youngest player in NBA history to pass the 20,000-point and 5,000-assist mark. James averaged 27.1 points, 7.9 rebounds, 6.2 assists, and 1.9 steals per game in the 2011–2012 season. He was named the league's MVP that year. James was an athlete at his peak. He led Miami into the playoffs as the second seed, and he was looking to make his fourth straight NBA Finals.

Miami played Carmelo Anthony and the New York Knicks in

the first round of the Eastern Conference Playoffs in 2012. James and the Heat easily took care of the Knicks in 5 games, winning the first 3 games before New York won a close 89–87 game to prevent the sweep. James battled with Anthony throughout the series, each scoring 27.8 points per game on average to lead their respective teams. However, James and the Heat had more talent from the start, and each of their wins in the series was by double digits.

In the second round, Miami squared off against the Indiana Pacers. Despite trailing to Indiana 2–1 in the series, the Heat won 3 straight games to take the series and reach the NBA Finals once again. James and Wade dominated the scoring against the Pacers, with James averaging 30 points per game and Wade finishing the series with 26.2 points per game. Mario Chalmers also played a key role for the Heat in the series, as Chris Bosh only played one game against the Pacers because of injury.

A seven-game series win over Boston then set up a matchup with the previous season's Western Conference runner-up, the Oklahoma City Thunder. Led by Kevin Durant, the Thunder were a young and exciting team that posed a challenge for the Heat. That challenge was evident right away, as Oklahoma City beat the Heat in Game 1.

James scored 30 points in the loss, but Thunder stars Kevin Durant and Russell Westbrook combined for 63 points and out-scored Miami in the second half by themselves. Some thought that James would be headed for yet another playoff failure against Durant and Westbrook's dynamic offensive attack. In Game 2, however, James finally took control. He had 32 points in a 100–96 win in Oklahoma City. With the series tied at one win apiece and heading back to Miami for three straight games, James and the Heat had the opportunity to win it all on their home court. Miami then won Game 3 to take back control of the series. James had 29 points and 14 rebounds in the win and helped the Heat hold off a late fourth-quarter rally from the Thunder.

In Game 4, James fought through cramps to lead Miami to a 104–98 win. Limping because of pain in his left leg, James still scored 26 points in the win. He also gave the Heat the lead with 2:51 left in the game with a 3-pointer that sealed Miami's 3–1 series lead. At the time, no team had ever blown a 3–1 series lead in the history of the NBA Finals.

With three chances to win one game for the NBA title, James had arguably his best game of the playoffs. In Game 5, he had 26 points, 11 rebounds, and 13 assists in a 121–106 win that clinched the NBA championship. That triple-double was a break-through moment in James's career. It showed that he was capable of playing at his absolute best when it mattered most. Finally, at 27 years old and in his ninth NBA season, LeBron James was an NBA champion. "My dream has become a reality now," James said, "and it's the best feeling I ever had."[37]

James was interviewed by ESPN's Doris Burke after the win. She asked James what it meant to finally win a championship, and he responded, "It means everything. I made a difficult deci-sion to leave Cleveland but I understood what my future was about … This is definitely where it pays off."[38]

Burke noted that James appeared to change his approach to basketball after experiencing failure in his first season with the Heat. James agreed that he had finally learned from his past failures:

> Losing in the Finals last year put me back into place. It humbled me a lot. I was able to go back to the basics. A lot of people had a lot to do with it but at the end of the day I just looked myself in the mirror and said, 'You need to be better.' Both on and off the floor, and I'm happy I was able to put myself and our team in a position to win.[39]

The victory meant more to James than just finally winning a championship. In the short NBA season, some had wondered if Durant had become the best player in the league. Even though James won the league MVP award, many—especially in Oklahoma City—wondered if Durant would surpass the "King." In the 2012 NBA Finals, though, James left no doubt about his dominance. He won the Finals MVP Award, averaged 26.8 points, 8 rebounds, 7.3 assists, and 1.7 steals per game while making 56.5 percent of the shots he took in the series. Most importantly, he saved his

James led the Heat to victory in the 2012 NBA Finals.

best game for when his team needed him most.

"It was a storybook season for him,"[40] Durant said to the media after Game 5. The King was finally crowned, but he was just getting started.

Back-to-Back Championships

The opening night of the 2012–2013 NBA season was a celebration for James and the Heat. Miami hosted the Boston Celtics. Before the game, the Heat raised their second NBA championship banner in franchise history. They then beat the Celtics, 120–107, with James totaling 26 points and 10 rebounds in the win. The Heat continued to find success in James's third season in Miami. In a stretch from February 2 to March 24, 2013, the Heat won 27 straight games. That was the third-longest winning streak in NBA history to that point and the longest in Heat franchise history.

James set an equally impressive individual achievement during that stretch. In the month of February, James shot 64.1 percent from the field, which is a very rare thing to do in professional basketball. *Sports Illustrated* called February 2013 a "month for the ages"[41] for James. He set an NBA record on February 12 in a 117–104 win over the Portland Trail Blazers. The win, which was Miami's 1,000th victory in franchise history, marked the sixth straight game where James scored at least 30 points and shot 60 percent from the field.

"I'm at a loss for words," James said after the game. "Like I say over and over, I know the history of the game. I know how many unbelievable players who came through the ranks, who paved the way for me and my teammates. And for me to be in the record books by myself with such a stat—any stat—it's big-time."[42]

James finished the regular season averaging 26.8 points, 8 rebounds, and 7.3 assists per game. His statistics were once again good enough to be named NBA MVP—his second straight MVP title and the fourth of his career. This time, however, he nearly became the first unanimous MVP in NBA history. Just 1 sportswriter out of a panel of 120 failed to give James a first-place vote, instead casting it for Carmelo Anthony. "It was probably a writer out of New York that didn't give me that vote," James joked when he accepted the award. "And we know the history between the Heat and the Knicks, so I get it."[43]

Despite having an amazing regular season, James remained focused on the postseason and a second straight NBA title. "My ultimate goal is to win an NBA championship," James said that May. "That's what I was brought here for. That's why I signed here as a free agent in 2010. It wasn't to win MVP trophies. It was to win a championship—and win multiple championships—and that's still my No. 1 priority."[44]

With a record of 66–16, Miami entered the playoffs as the top seed in the Eastern Conference. Miami swept the Milwaukee Bucks in the first round, and then took on Chicago in the Eastern Conference Semifinals. Without star Derrick Rose, Chicago struggled against the powerful Heat offensive attack, and Miami prevailed in five games.

The Eastern Conference Finals were a matchup between the Heat and the Indiana Pacers. In Game 1, James made a layup at the buzzer to beat the Pacers by a score of 103–102 in overtime. James had 30 points, 10 rebounds, and 10 assists—another playoff triple-double—in a wild game that featured 18 ties and 17 lead

London Gold

In the summer of 2012, James went to London to play in the Summer Olympics. James and a number of other NBA stars made up a U.S. squad hoping to repeat their gold medal success in 2008 in Beijing, China. Coached by Duke University basketball head coach Mike Krzyzewski, Team USA went undefeated in Olympic competition and won a second straight gold medal. James was a star for Team USA in the eight games the team played, though he and the team as a whole seemed to struggle a bit early in group play. James eventually broke out to score 20 points and help the United States squad come back against Lithuania in a 99–94 win. In the quarterfinals against Australia, he had a triple-double in the 119–86 win, finishing with 11 points, 14 rebounds, and 11 assists in the game. In the gold medal game against Spain, James scored 17 points in a 107–100 win to give Team USA another Olympic gold medal.

With the win in the gold medal game, James matched a feat only achieved by Michael Jordan at that time— winning the NBA MVP, NBA championship, NBA Finals MVP, and Olympic Gold medal.

changes. The teams alternated wins throughout the series, but the Heat came through in Game 7 with a commanding 23-point win to reach their third straight Finals with James on the team.

There, Miami took on the San Antonio Spurs, the same team James lost to in his first Finals appearance with Cleveland in 2007. Though Miami was gunning for their second straight title, they struggled against San Antonio's defense and trailed in the series 3–2 after 5 games. In Game 6, however, James broke out for a triple-double—his second of the series—and scored 16 points in the fourth quarter to help Miami force overtime. In the extra session, a pair of Ray Allen free throws sealed

James was successful in his title chase in Miami, winning two straight titles with the Heat.

the 103–100 win for Miami, tying the series and setting up a dramatic Game 7 back in front of their home crowd.

With a second straight NBA title on the line, James came through for Miami once more. In a close game until the very end, James scored a game-high 37 points and added 12 rebounds in a 95–88 Heat win to clinch another NBA title.

"I put a lot of work into it and to be able to come out here and (have) the results happen out on the floor is the ultimate," James said after the game, "The ultimate. I'm at a loss for words."[45]

James also won his second straight Finals MVP award. He averaged 25.3 points, 10.9 rebounds, 7 assists, and 2.3 steals per game throughout the series and once again saved his best performance for a series-clinching game. In his first three seasons in Miami, LeBron James had achieved everything he wanted to do when he made his infamous decision in the summer of 2010. He won two straight titles with some of his closest friends in the league and had helped build a basketball dynasty in Miami.

Speaking Out

As LeBron James's star continued to rise, he began to use his fame to draw attention to issues that mattered to him. He realized that he was able to reach millions of people—especially young men—thanks to his success on the basketball court, and he wanted to make his fans aware of social justice issues, including racism and police brutality.

In 2012, James led a Miami Heat protest after the death of Trayvon Martin, who was fatally shot on the streets of Sanford, Florida, by a neighborhood watch volunteer who thought the hoodie-wearing teenager looked dangerous. Martin had no weapon on him, but the watch member—George Zimmerman—claimed the 17-year-old looked threatening. Zimmerman was arrested but claimed self-defense. He was later found not guilty in a trial that sparked outrage nationwide. In the protest, James and the other members of the Heat wore hoodies and bowed their heads to conceal their faces in a striking image of solidarity many in the African American community rallied around. James also wrote "R.I.P. Trayvon Martin" on his sneakers, which he wore in a game against the Detroit Pistons.

In December 2014, James wore a shirt that said "I CAN'T BREATHE" before a game against the Brooklyn Nets at Barclays Center in Brooklyn, New York. The shirt was a reference to the death of an African American man named Eric Garner, who was killed in an altercation with New York City police in 2014. Video footage of the incident, in which Garner was subdued and suffocated using a chokehold that was considered illegal for officers to use, found its way online. Garner can be heard in the video gasping and saying "I can't breathe." He then lost consciousness and later died at a hospital. Despite the video evidence, the officer in question, Daniel Pantaleo, was not indicted on any charges as a result of Garner's death.

This death, as well as many other high-profile incidents between people of color and police departments across the country, drew nationwide protests. Many NBA players, including Kevin Garnett, Kyrie Irving, Deron Williams, and Derrick Rose, wore the shirts that week as well.

LeBron on Politics

Ever aware of his brand and the impact of his voice, LeBron James has hesitated to comment on politics in most situations in his career. His first sign of political affiliation came in 2008, when the *Cleveland Plain Dealer* reported James had donated $20,000 to the election campaign of Barack Obama. Later that year, James campaigned for Obama publicly at a concert event he hosted, which featured a performance from rapper Jay-Z. The "Last Chance for Change" event was held at Quicken Loans Arena and featured James encouraging those in attendance to vote in that year's presidential election. After that election, which Obama won, James stayed relatively quiet about other political events.

However, James continued to maintain a close relationship with Obama. The president played basketball when he was younger and remains an avid fan, so the two men connected over their shared love of the sport. That served as the foundation for a solid friendship. They have also bonded over their desire to help young people living in inner city neighborhoods.

After staying out of politics for years, James again supported a Democratic candidate for president in 2016. On October 3, about a month before Election Day, James publicly endorsed Hillary Clinton for president over Republican candidate Donald Trump. In an op-ed published by the website *Business Insider*, James said Clinton—the first major party female nominee for president in American history—would carry on President Obama's legacy in office. James wrote,

"It's not a Cavs thing," James told the media before the game. "It's a worldly thing."[46]

James had also spoken publicly about the deaths of other

When I look at this year's presidential race, it's clear which candidate believes the same thing. Only one person running truly understands the struggles of an Akron child born into poverty. And when I think about the kinds of policies and ideas the kids in my foundation need from our government, the choice is clear.

That candidate is Hillary Clinton.

I support Hillary because she will build on the legacy of my good friend, President Barack Obama. I believe in what President Obama has done for our country and support her commitment to continuing that legacy.[1]

1. LeBron James, "LeBron James: Why I'm Endorsing Hillary Clinton," *Business Insider*, October 2, 2016. www.businessinsider.com/lebron-james-why-endorsing-hillary-clinton-for-president-2016-9.

James had made multiple trips to the White House to celebrate NBA championships, but his friendship with Barack and Michelle Obama has extended beyond those visits.

young people of color at the hands of police in the previous months and years, including Mike Brown in Ferguson, Missouri, and Tamir Rice in Cleveland.

"It's just for us to make a [statement] to understand what we're going through as a society," James has said. "Obviously, as a society we have to do better. We have to be better for one another. It doesn't matter what race you are."[47]

During the summer of 2016, at ESPN's annual ESPY Awards, James and three other NBA stars—Carmelo Anthony, Chris Paul, and Dwyane Wade—took the stage in support of the growing Black Lives Matter movement that demanded more police accountability for violence against the African American community. Speaking after the other three, James said,

We all feel helpless and frustrated by the violence. We do. But that's not acceptable. It's time to look in the mirror and ask ourselves, "What are we doing to create change?" It's not about being a role model. It's not about our responsibility to a condition of activism. I know tonight, we'll honor Muhammad Ali, the G.O.A.T. To do his legacy any justice, let's use this moment as a call to action to all professional athletes to educate ourselves, explore these issues, speak up, use our influence, and renounce all violence. And most importantly go back to our communities. Invest our time, our resources. Help rebuild them. Help strengthen them. Help change them. We all have to do better. Thank you.[48]

James reinforced his belief that America must address the problem of violence in African American communities when he formally stated his support for Hillary Clinton in her 2016 presidential campaign. In an op-ed he wrote for *Business Insider*, he stated,

Finally, we must address the violence, of every kind, the African-American community is experiencing in our streets and seeing on our TVs. I believe rebuilding our communities by focusing on at-risk children is a significant part of the solution. However, I am not a politician, I don't know everything it will take finally to end the violence. But I do know we need a president who brings us together and keeps us unified. Policies and ideas that divide

As James has grown as a player and a person, he has become more outspoken about topics beyond basketball, commenting on social issues and endorsing Hillary Clinton for president in 2016.

us more are not the solution. We must all stand together — no matter where we are from or the color of our skin.[49]

As James has matured and become more comfortable with his status as a celebrity and influencer of public opinion, he has used that role to better express his feelings about important political and social issues impacting the country. No longer worried about what could happen to his shoe deal or if people might not like him, he has taken steps to better the community through his various foundations and reinforce those actions by publicly supporting initiatives and political candidates he feels can make a difference in the lives of at-risk people of color who were born into similar situations he found himself in as a young child in Akron. James had grown up a lot during his time in Miami, and by 2014, he was ready to go back home.

Chapter Five

Coming Home

With two straight NBA titles under his belt, LeBron James still was not satisfied. As the 2013–2014 season got underway, the rumblings had already begun: James could once again become a free agent after the season. Some speculated that James would set himself up for another *Decision*-style dramatic summer after the season ended.

Sure enough, after the 2014 season, which saw the Heat lose to the Spurs in the NBA Finals, James opted out of his contract with the Heat. The news broke on June 25. By the next week, reports surfaced that James's agent Rich Paul was meeting with a number of teams interested in James. Among the teams interested were the Heat and, surprisingly, the Cleveland Cavaliers.

Despite everything that happened in Cleveland after James left the Cavs, there was hope from some that the team would one day welcome James back to win an NBA title before the superstar retired. The groundwork for a return to Cleveland happened well before the summer of 2014. Even as James was winning in Miami and the Cavs were struggling without him, the relationship between James and those he left behind in Cleveland was changing. Before a game against Cleveland in 2012, James even said he would be willing to come back to the Cavs someday. "I think it would be great," he said on February 17, 2012. "If I decide to come back, hopefully the fans will accept me."[50]

Cavaliers owner Dan Gilbert was reportedly so angry at James

Even after harsh words and burning jerseys when James left, some fans in Cleveland still hoped he would return one day. That day came sooner than many of them thought.

when he first left that he refused to speak his name in meetings for more than a year after he published his infamous letter following *The Decision*. By 2013, though, even he began to soften his stance on James, posting this statement on Twitter on March 20 of that year: "Cleveland Cavaliers' young talent makes our future very bright. Clearly, LeBron's is as well. Time for everyone to focus on the road ahead."[51]

James and the Cavs had a better relationship as time passed. The Cavs gave James and the rest of the Heat food from Swensons, his favorite burger restaurant in Akron, when Miami played in Cleveland in November 2013. The team also thought of James when the Cavs retired the jersey of Zydrunas Ilgauskas, one of James's favorite teammates during his early years in Cleveland. James came back to Cleveland for the ceremony because team officials held the ceremony on a night when James would be off.

The moves were small, but some in Cleveland were hopeful that James could find a way to return to the Cavs. With a

The "Air Conditioning Game"

Game 1 of the 2014 NBA Finals between the Heat and the Spurs was one of the strangest games in NBA history. The air conditioning in San Antonio's AT&T Center broke, with temperatures inside the building reaching as high as 90 degrees Fahrenheit (32.2 degrees Celsius) during the game. Players were seen putting ice packs on their necks during timeouts while fans tried to cool themselves in the stands.

Players on both teams struggled in the rising heat and humidity, but James was hit hardest. He had severe leg cramps and had to leave the game. James had 25 points in 33 minutes but played only 5 minutes of the fourth quarter. The Spurs outscored the Heat 36–17 in the game's final 12 minutes to win 110–95 and take the lead in the series. James's leg locked up completely, and he had to be carried off the court by teammates after the game.

"I was losing a lot [of fluids] throughout the game. It was extremely hot in the building, you know, both teams, fans, everybody could feel it," James said after the game. "It was an unusual circumstance," he continued. "I never played in a building like that."[1]

1. Quoted in Royce Young, "Air Conditioning Goes Out in Game 1," ESPN.com, June 6, 2014. www.espn.com/nba/playoffs/2014/story/_/id/11039853/2014-nba-finals-lebron-james-exits-game-1-loss-thigh-cramp-c-fails.

number of talented young players on Cleveland's roster due to their struggles and subsequent high draft picks since James left, things were starting to look up in Cleveland. The bright future ahead of the Cavs made the team an attractive option for free agents, including James.

The End in Miami

James's final season in Miami was nearly as impressive as his first three with the Heat. On March 3, 2014, James broke a Heat franchise record with a career-high 61-point game against the Charlotte Bobcats. Miami dealt with injuries to its "Big Three" and much of its supporting cast during this season, but James still thrived. He finished the regular season averaging 27.1 points, 6.9 rebounds, and 6.4 assists per game, and he shot 56.7 percent from the field that season.

Miami finished the season 54–28, which led the Southeast Division for a fourth consecutive season. They swept the Bobcats in the first round of the playoffs, and they beat the Brooklyn Nets in 5 games in the next round, thanks to a career postseason record of 49 points from James in a Game 4 win. Miami then beat the Pacers in six games to become just the fourth team in NBA history to reach four straight NBA Finals.

During the first game of the NBA Finals, the air conditioning broke in the Spurs' arena, which affected everyone's play, especially James, who missed time because of leg cramps. The Spurs went on to win the game and take the lead in the series.

The "Air Conditioning Game" set the stage for a series where the Heat would come up short against San Antonio in a variety of ways despite James's strong play. In Game 2, James scored 35 points and shot 64 percent from the floor. He averaged 28.2 points, 7.8 rebounds, and 2 steals per game in the series, but Tim Duncan and the Spurs won the title in 5 games to end Miami's hopes for a third straight championship.

Not only was James's remarkable four-year stay in Miami bookended by failure in the NBA Finals, but also fans soon learned that his time in South Beach was to be bookended by playing for his hometown team in Cleveland.

In His Own Words

After the 2013–2014 season was over, the world was left once again wondering where James would play basketball. This time, though, he took a decidedly different approach to his announcement concerning where he would play. On July 11, 2014, in a first-person essay written along with Lee Jenkins, James announced to the readers of *Sports Illustrated* that he was "coming home" to Cleveland:

> *Before anyone ever cared where I would play basketball, I was a kid from Northeast Ohio. It's where I walked. It's where I ran. It's where I cried. It's where I bled. It holds a special place in my heart. People there have seen me grow up. I sometimes feel like I'm their son. Their passion can be overwhelming. But it drives me. I want to give them hope when I can. I want to inspire them when I can. My relationship with Northeast Ohio is bigger than basketball. I didn't realize that four years ago. I do now.[52]*

James appreciated the region that he felt made him who he was, and he believed he could give back to the people of that region by winning a championship with them and for them. He had matured in his time away from the Cavaliers, and it showed in the way he announced his return. James said there would be no "press conference" or "party" to celebrate this time. "After this," he wrote, "it's time to get to work." He continued,

> *When I left Cleveland, I was on a mission. I was seeking championships, and we won two. But Miami already knew that feeling. Our city hasn't had that feeling in a long, long, long time. My goal is still to win as many titles as possible, no question. But what's most important for me is bringing one trophy back to Northeast Ohio.[53]*

James signed a two-year deal with the Cavaliers. The month before, just days after Cleveland took Andrew Wiggins with the first overall pick in the 2014 NBA draft, James met with Dan Gilbert face-to-face for the first time since 2010. With James back in Cleveland, the team made more moves to improve. On August 23, the Cavs traded Wiggins along with a pick they got

Cleveland moved quickly to bring in new talent to help Kyrie Irving after James announced his return to the Cavs, trading for Kevin Love.

from Miami in James's sign-and-trade for standout power forward Kevin Love. Along with up-and-coming star Kyrie Irving and a young group of Cavs thrilled to have the game's best player on the roster, Cleveland felt they were close to finally winning a title.

Family First

In announcing his return to Cleveland in 2014, James said it was his family that made him realize the importance of home and of bringing positive things to the place he loves:

> *I always believed that I'd return to Cleveland and finish my career there. I just didn't know when. After the season, free agency wasn't even a thought. But I have two boys and my wife, Savannah, is pregnant with a girl. I started thinking about what it would be like to raise my family in my hometown. I looked at*

other teams, but I wasn't going to leave Miami for anywhere except Cleveland. The more time passed, the more it felt right. This is what makes me happy.[54]

Although James is a superstar on and off the basketball court, perhaps his greatest satisfaction comes from being a father. On October 6, 2004, James and his longtime girlfriend, Savannah Brinson, had a child together—LeBron James Jr. He credits his son with helping him mature and making him more aware of the kind of man he wants to be. James wants to be a good father and a solid presence in his son's life. He has talked openly about how being a father has enlightened him:

James married his high school sweetheart, Savannah Brinson. As of 2016, the couple has three children. Family is very important to James.

It's great. Sometimes in the past when I played something might make me lose focus, or I would go home after a game where I thought I could have played better and I would let it hang over my head for a long time when it shouldn't.

But now, being a parent, I go home and see my son and I forget about any mistake I ever made or the reason I'm upset. I get home

Appreciating His Mother

James always appreciated his mother, but becoming a father himself allowed him to better understand what she went through raising him so young and in such a difficult situation. As a father, James has said he appreciates even more the sacrifices his mother made to raise him. "Now that I have a son," he said, "I have no idea how she did it by herself because I couldn't do it by myself. She taught me through all the trials and tribulations. She's by far my greatest influence. She gets all the credit. I don't know how, but she did it."[1]

James credits his mother with being his biggest inspiration as a parent, especially because his father was not a part of his life. He has stated that he wants to be the father he never had as a kid and that he wants to pass on the lessons his mother taught him to his own children.

1. Quoted in Associated Press, "AP Interview: LeBron James _ Beyond his Years, Beyond the Hype," ESPN.com, December 10, 2005. www.espn.com/espn/wire/_/section/nba/id/2254792.

and my son is smiling or he comes running to me. It has just made me grow as an individual and grow as a man.[55]

During the 2007 postseason, James and Brinson welcomed a second son, Bryce Maximus James, who was born on June 14. James and Brinson were married on September 14, 2013, in San Diego, California. On June 19, 2014, news broke that James and his wife were expecting a third child. Their daughter, Zhuri James, was born on October 22, 2014.

Running into the "Dubs"

The 2014–2015 NBA season featured two compelling storylines—one in each conference. The first was James's return to

Cleveland in the Eastern Conference. The other was the rise of the Golden State Warriors in the Western Conference. Led by point guard Stephen (Steph) Curry, the dynamic offensive attack of the Warriors—sometimes called the "Dubs"—stunned opponents. Curry and Klay Thompson were so effective at three-point shooting that they became known as the "Splash Brothers," and both players were All-Star starters for the Western Conference that season. Steph Curry was named the league's MVP, and many thought the Warriors were destined to become champions that spring.

Meanwhile, James's return to the Cavs reinvigorated the team under head coach David Blatt. Cleveland had two long winning streaks—8 games from late November to early December and 12 games in January to early February—to put the Cavs atop the Central Division. Cleveland went 53–29 in the 2014–2015 season, but James struggled at times. He missed two weeks in January with multiple injuries, including spraining his lower back and his left knee. It was the longest stretch of games he had missed in his career.

Cleveland made it to the playoffs that season, which marked the first time the team had done so since James left for Miami. In the playoffs, Cleveland swept the Boston Celtics in the first round. The Cavs matched up with the Chicago Bulls in the second round, and James provided some last-second magic in Game 4. With the game tied at 84, he took an inbound pass from Matthew Dellavedova and hit a shot at the buzzer to give Cleveland the win and tie the series at 2 wins apiece.

After the game, James said he drew up the game-winning play. "To be honest, the play that was drawn up, I scratched it," he said. "I told coach, 'Just get me the ball. We're either going to go into overtime, or I'm going to win it for us.' It was that simple."[56]

Cleveland won the series in six games and moved on to face the Atlanta Hawks in the Eastern Conference Finals. There, James and the Cavs easily handled the Hawks in a four-game sweep to reach the NBA Finals. James became the first player since Bill Russell in the 1960s to make five straight NBA Finals.

Cleveland's opponent was Steph Curry's Golden State Warriors. The lone meeting between the Cavs and Warriors during the regular season was a 110–99 Cleveland win, but this time, injuries had taken their toll on the Cavs. Irving and Love—two key pieces for the Cavs offense— missed most of the Finals with injuries. In a somewhat ironic twist of fate, James once again lacked a strong supporting cast but did what he could to try to lead the Cavaliers to an NBA title.

The Warriors were simply too much, however. Their dynamic offense was firing on all cylinders against a Cavs team unable to keep up, with players such as Timofey Mozgov and Matthew Dellavedova forced to play significant minutes.

James did everything he could to help his team, putting on his best Finals performance to that point. Despite losing Game 1, James led Cleveland to 2 straight wins to take an early lead in the series. James scored 39 points in the team's 95–93 Game 2 win, and he accounted for 40 points, 12 rebounds, and 8 assists in a 96–91 Game 3 win. Even with those outstanding individual performances from James, the Warriors prevailed in the next three games to win the series and keep him from bringing Cleveland a championship once more. Even in the loss, James was still considered for the Finals MVP award. He averaged 35.8 points, 13.3 rebounds, and 8.8 assists in the 6-game series. However, Andre Iguodala won the award for the Warriors instead of James, who now had a long summer ahead of him to think about what went wrong in Cleveland once again.

LeBron James: Coach Killer?

James's second season back in Cleveland was, for a while, much smoother than his first. Cleveland cruised through the regular season's early months. After an opening-night loss at Chicago, the Cavs won eight straight and quickly established themselves as the best team in the Eastern Conference. However, the team's head coach, David Blatt, and James appeared to have a strained relationship, and rumors swirled that other players were also having problems with the coach, despite their record.

On January 24, 2016, just 41 games into the season, Blatt was fired by the team's general manager David Griffin, and he was replaced by top assistant coach Tyronn Lue. Reports of leadership issues and some errors in game management surfaced after the firing, suggesting that, even though the 30–11 Cavs were the best team in the East, they lost faith in their coach.

Sources for the Associated Press and ESPN reported that James was not directly involved or consulted when the decision was made to fire Blatt, but many thought James had actively made it known he wanted Lue to coach the team.

"I didn't talk to any of the players before this decision," Griffin said to the Associated Press at the time. "It's really critical to me for everybody to understand this is my decision. This is our basketball staff's decision … I'm not taking a poll."[57]

Despite being at the center of a controversy that rattled the NBA, the Cavs continued to cruise through the regular season. They finished the second half of the season 27–14 under Lue to finish with the best record in the Eastern Conference and take the top seed overall in the playoffs.

Cleveland reached the NBA Finals in James's first season back with the Cavs, but the team ultimately lost to Golden State in six games.

James, however, continued to face scrutiny from fans and the media about how he handled the firing of David Blatt and some things he posted on social media that seemed to be directed at teammates. Many thought that James was getting the reputation of being a "coach killer," or someone who could use his power to get a coach fired if he did not like what was happening with a team.

However, ESPN reporter Brian Windhorst noted that only two coaches had been fired in James's career while he was on their team. The first, Paul Silas, was fired from Cleveland during an ownership change and when James was in just his second season. The firing of Blatt came 11 years later. Though James denied he had anything to do with the move, many in sports were skeptical of his denial. Windhorst's article noted how outspoken James can be and that, at times, he can be difficult to coach:

> Erik Spoelstra [James's coach in Miami] had some of the most trying days of his career in his first months as James' coach in 2010. Mike Krzyzewski considered cutting James after his first training camp with Team USA in 2006. But both coaches ultimately experienced huge success with James; Spoelstra won two titles and Krzyzewski won two gold medals.[58]

As the attention mounted and his every action was questioned, James knew he had to deliver a title to Cleveland sooner rather than later.

The Path to the Finals

Cleveland headed to the playoffs in 2016 poised to make a repeat trip to the Finals—so, too, did the Golden State Warriors. In fact, Curry and his teammates had established themselves as one of the best teams in NBA history. They won an NBA-record 73 games in the regular season, breaking a record set by the 1996 Chicago Bulls, who were led by one of the most famous players in NBA history, Michael Jordan.

The first three rounds of the 2016 playoffs were perhaps some of the most comfortable of James's career, leading up to what seemed to be an inevitable matchup with Curry and the Warriors. Cleveland lost just two games in the first three rounds—both against the Toronto Raptors in the Eastern Conference Finals. Cleveland swept Detroit in the opening round and Atlanta in the Eastern Conference Semifinals, but the Cavs faced a tied series

Social Media Struggles

James's use of social media has allowed him to connect with his fans, but it has also led to controversy at times, especially when the meaning behind his posts are left up to interpretation. For example, during the period of heightened attention after the firing of David Blatt, James's messages on Twitter and Instagram drew criticism from some who felt he was calling out his teammates in a public way, but James brushed it off as him motivating himself, not others. "They're for the educated mind," James said. "So if you have an educated mind, they hit home for you ... It's nothing between the lines, it's just life." James also said he has stopped caring about what other people think of him, which can be difficult to do when you maintain a presence on social media platforms:

Twitter hasn't been around that long, I'm kind of old. I don't know. I think the other question is when I stopped caring about what other people think. I can remember that, it was my second year in Miami. I just stopped, it became too much where I was worried about what other people think instead of just making the main thing the main thing, and that's just playing the game of basketball that I love and being happy about being in this situation. I'm a blessed kid from—you guys know the story—40 miles south of here. I've got a beautiful family, beautiful teammates, and this game of basketball has brought me so much, so the outside noises just really don't affect me.[1]

Each postseason, James stays off of social media to focus on basketball. His yearly social media blackout has become something that is reported on by news organizations throughout the world of sports.

1. Quoted in Dave McMenamin, "LeBron James Doesn't Mind if Social Media Posts Cause Conflict," ESPN.com, March 7, 2016. www.espn.com/nba/story/_/id/14921113/lebron-james-cleveland-cavaliers-likes-express-beautiful-mind-social-media.

against the Raptors, despite two blowout wins at home in the first two games. James and the Cavs bounced back after Game 4, winning the final 2 games of the series by large margins to clinch their second straight trip to the NBA Finals. It was far from James's second straight trip. By 2016, he had reached the NBA Finals seven years in a row.

An Amazing Comeback

The 2016 NBA Finals will likely go down in history as one of the most remarkable seven-game series ever played between two teams at their peak. It started, however, looking like it would be no contest at all. Golden State cruised to double-digit wins at home to take an early 2–0 series lead. Game 3, however, was a blowout in Cleveland's favor. James had 32 points in the 120–90 win. The Warriors responded in Game 4, taking control of the Finals with a 108–97 win that put them on the brink of their second straight NBA title.

History was against James and the Cavs. No team had ever blown a 3–1 lead in the NBA Finals, let alone the best regular season team in NBA history. Many wrote off the Cavs and suggested there was no way to beat Golden State in three straight games. The Warriors had lost just one playoff game at home all season and—until the Western Conference Finals against Oklahoma City—had not lost two straight games all season.

All those numbers, however, only set the stage for one of the most impressive comebacks in NBA history. With James leading the charge, Cleveland won Game 5 in Oakland, California, 112–97, with James scoring 41 points to go along with his 16 rebounds and 7 assists. Game 6 was back in Cleveland, where James had another 41-point game in a Cleveland win. His impressive performance was aided by 23 points from Kyrie Irving, and a double-double from Tristan Thompson helped even the series at 3 wins apiece.

Game 7 was one of the most anticipated games in NBA history. It was played on Sunday, June 19, 2016. Either Golden State would win its second straight title and cement itself as one of the best teams in NBA history or LeBron James would finally bring a championship to his hometown. The game was close throughout. Cleveland led by one point after the first quarter, but Golden State went into halftime with a lead in front of the team's home crowd in the Oracle Arena.

A back-and-forth third quarter set up a tense final 12 minutes. In arguably the most important quarter of LeBron James's career, he started with a basket inside to give Cleveland the lead. The game stayed close in the fourth quarter, setting up a dramatic finish. A big three-pointer from Golden State felt inevitable; it was what the team had become known for. However, Curry missed three shots beyond the three-point arc in the final two minutes. The game's defining moment came with the game tied at 89. Golden State's Andre Iguodala picked up a loose ball and ran down the court on a breakaway, ready to put up a layup that would have given Golden State the lead with 1:50 left to play. James sprinted back on defense, leaping at just the right time to block the layup as it was on the backboard to keep the score tied.

Cleveland came back down the court with a chance to take the lead. Kyrie Irving then broke that 89–89 tie with a 3-pointer with 53 seconds left to give Cleveland a lead they would not give up. James made a free throw with 11 seconds left on the clock to finish with 11 fourth-quarter points. The Warriors did not score again, and that was it. Golden State had blown a 3–1 lead in the NBA Finals. LeBron James and the Cleveland Cavaliers were NBA Champions.

A Hometown Hero

James finished the game with yet another triple-double: 27 points, 11 rebounds, and 11 assists. His series average of 29.7 points, 11.3 rebounds, and 8.9 assists was good enough for his third career Finals MVP award. He said even with all the pressure on him to deliver a title to Cleveland, his focus was only on basketball.

"The game always gives back to people that are true to the game," he said. "I've watched it. I know the history of the game, and I was just calm. I was calm."[59]

James remained calm during the game, but he let his emotions out after it was over. He had achieved exactly what he set out to do when he returned to the Cavs. He finally brought a championship to the region where he grew up. "I came back for a reason," James said. "I came back to bring a championship to our city."[60]

As a man who grew up in Ohio, James understood what the win meant to Cleveland and the entire region around it. The win was the city of Cleveland's first championship since 1964, making it a huge milestone in the history of professional sports in the city.

James fought back tears while he conducted his postgame media session, clutching the NBA championship trophy while wearing one of the nets the team cut down from the Oracle Arena. He was so excited about the victory parade that would be held in Cleveland he even invited the media: "It's going to be the biggest party that Cleveland has ever seen. If you guys still have a little money left over in your budget, you guys better make a trip to Cleveland and get a little piece of it."[61]

James was right; the parade was a huge celebration. It was estimated that 1.3 million people descended on downtown Cleveland to

James was the focal point of Cleveland's epic comeback in the 2016 NBA Finals.

watch the parade make its way through the streets. Cavs fans came out in huge numbers to celebrate the win and to cheer on the team that made it possible, especially James. Only a few years before, fans were burning his jersey. Now, they had welcomed him back with open arms and crowned him not just the NBA's king, but their hometown hero.

A Living Legend

At age 31, James had finally achieved every goal he had set for himself. He had taken care of his mother, created a family for himself, and won NBA titles with two different teams. The superstar had learned much about himself, how to fight through criticism, and how find his own way. Most importantly, he found success everywhere he played—even in Cleveland, a city many residents thought would be cursed with sports failure. More than a decade into his NBA career, James might

James delivered Cleveland's first sports title since 1964 and took home the NBA Finals MVP trophy again in 2016.

Success Off the Court

In addition to James's success on the basketball court, he has also found success off of it, especially in recent years. His lifetime endorsement deal with Nike made headlines in 2015, but that is far from his only business partnership. James has also signed endorsement deals with Samsung electronics and the Coca-Cola Company, which frequently features him in adds for Sprite.

James is also an investor who has backed businesses such as the custom-made pizza chain Blaze Pizza. In late 2015, James chose to leave his partnership with McDonald's to become part of Blaze Pizza's advertising campaigns.

James has found himself in the spotlight beyond just basketball and business. He has hosted both *Saturday Night Live* and the ESPY Awards. In 2015, he played himself in the R-rated comedy *Trainwreck*, which starred Amy Schumer. His performance in the film was popular with critics and fans alike, and it opened the door to the possibility of more big-screen appearances by James in the future.

not be the most dominant or the best player in the game, but he has become so much more: a living legend in the modern sports world.

To some of his harsher critics, James's legacy may be that of losing in multiple NBA Finals. Others, however, will be reminded of words he wrote when he announced his return to Cleveland two years before he led the Cavs to a championship: "In Northeast Ohio, nothing is given. Everything is earned. You work for what you have."[62]

James has taken that lesson to heart. He has worked for everything in his career, and that work has undoubtedly paid off, making him one of the greatest players in the history of basketball.

Notes

Chapter One: The Young King James

1. Quoted in Jack McCallum, "You Gotta Carry That Weight." *Sports Illustrated*, October 27, 2003, p. 74.

2. Quoted in Associated Press, "AP Interview: LeBron James _ Beyond his Years, Beyond the Hype," ESPN.com, December 10, 2005. www.espn.com/espn/wire/_/section/nba/id/2254792.

3. Quoted in Eli Saslow, "Lost Stories of LeBron, Part 1," ESPN.com, October 17, 2013. www.espn.com/nba/story/_/id/9825052/how-lebron-james-life-changed-fourth-grade-espn-magazine.

4. Quoted in David Lee Morgan Jr., *LeBron James: The Rise of a Star*. Cleveland, OH: Gray & Company Publishers, 2003, p. 33.

5. Quoted in Morgan, *LeBron James,* p. 86.

6. Quoted in Morgan, *LeBron James,* p. 39.

7. Quoted in Morgan, *LeBron James,* p. 60.

8. Quoted in Terry Pluto, "LeBron James, Once a Lanky Kid, Has Come a Long Way in the NBA." *Akron Beacon Journal*, April 20, 2004.

9. Scott Fowler, "Still in High School, James has EBay, NBA Circling." *Knight Ridder/Tribune News Service*, December 10, 2002.

10. Quoted in Morgan, *LeBron James,* p. 87.

11. Quoted in Morgan, *LeBron James,* p. 96.

12. Quoted in Morgan, *LeBron James,* p. 12.

13. Quoted in Morgan, *LeBron James,* p. 125.

14. Quoted in Ryan Jones, *King James: Believe the Hype: The LeBron James Story.* New York, NY: St. Martin's Press, 2003, p. 184.

Chapter Two: King of Cleveland

15. Michelle Kaufman, "At 17, LeBron James Ponders His NBA Future." *Knight Ridder/Tribune News Service,* December 2, 2002.

16. Quoted in Roger Gordon, *Tales from the Cleveland Cavaliers: The Rookie Season of LeBron James.* Champaign, IL: Sports Publishing LLC, 2004, p. 133.

17. Ron Schwane, "LeBron, Stoudemire Among Five Added to Olympic Hoops Team," *USA Today,* May 14, 2004. usatoday30.usatoday.com/sports/olympics/athens/news/2004-05-14-mens-hoop-team_x.htm.

18. Quoted in Sean Deveney, "Crystal Baller: LeBron James's Uncanny Ability to See What's Coming is Keeping Him a Step Ahead of the Competition." *The Sporting News,* December 20, 2004.

19. Howard Beck, "Cavaliers Sinking, Despite James's Efforts," *New York Times,* April 15, 2005. www.nytimes.com/2005/04/15/sports/basketball/cavaliers-sinking-despite-jamess-efforts.html.

20. "LeBron James Takes Over Game 5!," YouTube video, 3:20, posted by NBA, June 1, 2007. www.youtube.com/watch?v=d1Px-jPm_TU.

Chapter Three: *The Decision*

21. Quoted in Nick Friedell, "James Defends Not Shaking Hands," ESPN.com, August 12, 2009. www.espn.com/chicago/news/story?id=4392572.

22. Quoted in Friedell, "James Defends Not Shaking Hands."

23. Quoted in Henry Abbott, "LeBron James' Decision: The Transcript," ESPN.com, July 9, 2010. www.espn.com/blog/truehoop/post/_/id/17853/lebron-james-decision-the-transcript.

24. Quoted in Rich Thomaselli, "How LeBron's Entourage Got His 'Decision' on ESPN," *AdvertisingAge*, July 12, 2010. adage.com/article/news/lebron-s-entourage-decision-espn/144882/.

25. Quoted in Thomaselli, "How LeBron's Entourage Got His 'Decision' on ESPN."

26. Quoted in Thomaselli, "How LeBron's Entourage Got His 'Decision' on ESPN."

27. "Cleveland: Fans React to LeBron's Decision to Leave the Cavs - July 2010," YouTube video, 5:27, posted by News 5 Cleveland, July 8, 2010. www.youtube.com/watch?v=tTgNlIEY_fw.

28. Quoted in "Letter from Cavs Owner Dan Gilbert," ESPN.com, December 13, 2010. www.espn.com/nba/news/story?id=5365704.

29. Quoted in Brian Windhorst, "LeBron James Talks Contract," ESPN.com, February 1, 2013. www.espn.com/new-york/nba/story/_/id/8905486/lebron-james-think-paid-value-current-cba.

30. Quoted in "Heat Stars Sign Six-Year Deals,"

ESPN.com, July 10, 2010. www.espn.com/nba/news/story?id=5368003.

31. Quoted in Brian Windhorst, "How the Cavs Got LeBron Back Home," ESPN.com, September 14, 2014. www.espn.com/nba/story/_/id/11588922/the-three-year-plan-lure-lebron-james-back-cleveland.

32. Quoted in Sports Network, "Heat Throw Party to Introduce James, Wade, Bosh," *Toronto Sun*, July 9, 2010. www.torontosun.com/sports/basketball/2010/07/09/14667666.html.

33. Quoted in Associated Press, "Miami Heat Fans Welcome LeBron James, Dwyane Wade, Chris Bosh to AmericanAirlines Arena," *New York Daily News*, July 10, 2010. www.nydailynews.com/sports/basketball/miami-heat-fans-lebron-james-dwyane-wade-chris-bosh-americanairlines-arena-article-1.464464.

34. Quoted in "On Stage Interview with Wade, Bosh and James - July 9, 2010," NBA.com, July 9, 2010. www.nba.com/heat/news/on_stage_interview_wade_bosh_james_2010_07_10.html/.

35. Quoted in Howard Beck, "Shift in Talent Fortifies Elite Teams," *New York Times*, October 25, 2010. www.nytimes.com/2010/10/26/sports/basketball/26stern.html?_r=1&ref=basketball.

Chapter Four: Winning in Miami

36. Quoted in Charles Hollis, "Hot Corner: With NBA Title at Stake, LeBron James Was a Big Flop," AL.com,

June 15, 2011. www.al.com/sports/index.ssf/2011/06/hot_corner_with_nba_title_at_s.html.

37. Quoted in Johnny Ludden, "LeBron James Captures His First Championship as Heat Win NBA Finals," Yahoo! Sports. June 21, 2012. sports.yahoo.com/news/nba--lebron-james-captures-his-first-championship-as-heat-win-nba-finals.html.

38. Quoted in Fred Kerber, "LeBron, Heat Win NBA Title," *New York Post*, June 22, 2012. nypost.com/2012/06/22/lebron-heat-win-nba-title/.

39. "2012 NBA Finals: LeBron James Championship Interview," YouTube video, 1:29, posted by TheNBANation, June 21, 2012. www.youtube.com/watch?v=D9btNuf67iA.

40. Quoted in Ludden, "LeBron James Captures His First NBA Championship."

41. Quoted in Rob Mahoney, "LeBron James' Month for the Ages," *Sports Illustrated*, February 28, 2013. www.si.com/nba/point-forward/2013/02/28/lebron-james-miami-heat-february.

42. Quoted in Associated Press, "LeBron James Sets NBA Record in Heat's Win Against Blazers," ESPN.com, February 13, 2013. www.espn.com/nba/recap/_/id/400278490.

43. Quoted in Associated Press, "James Wins 4th Kia MVP Award in Near Unanimous Vote," NBA.com, May 6, 2013. www.nba.com/2013/news/05/05/lebron-james-wins-mvp.ap/.

44. Quoted in Associated Press, "James Wins 4th Kia MVP Award."

45. Quoted in Associated Press, "LeBron James Named MVP as Miami Heat Wins Second Straight Title," Cleveland.com, June 21, 2013. www.cleveland.com/lebron/index.ssf/2013/06/miami_heat_beats_san_antonio_s.html.

46. Quoted in Dave McMenamin and Mike Mazzeo, "LeBron, Irving in 'I Can't Breathe' Tees," ESPN.com, December 9, 2014. www.espn.com/nba/story/_/id/12001456/lebron-james-kyrie-irving-cleveland-cavaliers-kevin-garnett-deron-williams-brooklyn-nets-wear-breathe-shirt-reference-eric-garner.

47. Quoted in McMenamin and Mazzeo, "LeBron, Irving in 'I Can't Breathe' Tees."

48. Quoted in Matthew Dessem, "Watch the Black Lives Matter Speech Four NBA Stars Gave at the ESPY Awards," *Slate*, July 13, 2016. www.slate.com/blogs/browbeat/2016/07/13/nba_stars_opened_the_espys_with_a_black_lives_matter_speech.html.

49. LeBron James, "LeBron James: Why I'm Endorsing Hillary Clinton," *Business Insider*, October 2, 2016. www.businessinsider.com/lebron-james-why-endorsing-hillary-clinton-for-president-2016-9.

Chapter Five: Coming Home

50. Quoted in Windhorst, "How the Cavs Got LeBron Back Home."

51. Quoted in Windhorst, "How the Cavs Got LeBron Back Home."

52. LeBron James, "LeBron: I'm Coming Back to Cleveland," *Sports Illustrated*, July 11, 2014. www.si.com/nba/2014/07/11/lebron-james-cleveland-cavaliers.

53. James, "I'm Coming Back to Cleveland."

54. James, "I'm Coming Back to Cleveland."

55. Quoted in Associated Press, "Beyond his Years, Beyond the Hype."

56. Quoted in AFP, "LeBron James Hits Buzzer Beater as Cavaliers Edge Bulls," Yahoo! Sports, May 11, 2015. sports.yahoo.com/news/james-hits-buzzer-beater-lift-cavs-past-bulls-230515268--nba.html.

57. Quoted in ESPN.com News Services, "David Blatt Fired as Cavaliers Coach; Tyronn Lue to Take Over Team," ESPN.com, January 24, 2016. www.espn.com/nba/story/_/id/14627529/david-blatt-fired-cleveland-cavaliers-coach.

58. Quoted in Brian Windhorst, "For NBA Coaches, Is LeBron James Really a Big Professional Hazard?," ESPN.com, January 28, 2106. www.espn.com/nba/story/_/id/14663758/windhorst-lebron-coach-killer.

59. Quoted in Scott Cacciola, "Cavaliers Defeat Warriors to Win Their First N.B.A. Title," *New York Times*, June 19, 2016. www.nytimes.com/2016/06/20/sports/basketball/golden-state-warriors-cleveland-cavaliers-nba-championship.html.

60. Quoted in Cacciola, "Cavaliers Defeat Warriors."

61. Quoted in Cacciola, "Cavaliers Defeat Warriors."

62. James, "I'm Coming Back to Cleveland."

LeBron James Year by Year

1984

LeBron Raymone James is born in Akron, Ohio, on December 30.

1994

James plays organized basketball for the first time.

2002

James appears on the cover of *Sports Illustrated*.

2003

James is involved in two potential scandals involving a Hummer and throwback jerseys, signs a multimillion-dollar deal with Nike, and is the first player chosen in the NBA draft.

2004

James is named Rookie of the Year in the NBA and is named to the U.S. men's Olympic basketball team; James and Savannah Brinson welcome their first child, LeBron James Jr.

2006

James leads the Cavaliers in his first playoff experience.

2007

Cleveland reaches the NBA Finals for the first time in James's career; James's son Bryce Maximus is born.

2010

James joins the Miami Heat and announces his plan during the ESPN special, *The Decision*.

2011

James and the Heat lose in the NBA Finals to the Dallas Mavericks.

2012

The Heat win the NBA title, and James is named the NBA Finals MVP; James helps Team USA win a gold medal at the London Olympics.

2013

The Heat repeat as NBA champions, James wins his second Finals MVP award, and James marries his longtime girlfriend, Savannah Brinson.

2014

James makes it to his sixth straight NBA Finals but loses; he announces return to Cleveland in July and welcomes his daughter Zhuri in October.

2015

The Cavaliers lose to the Golden State Warriors in the NBA Finals.

2016

James leads the Cavs in a historic comeback to win the NBA title.

For More Information

Books

Ciovacco, Justine. *LeBron James: NBA Champion*. New York, NY: Rosen Publishing, 2016.
Ciovacco's account of James's life details the events that made him the man he is today—from his difficult childhood to his relationship with his fans.

Donnelly, Patrick. *The Best NBA Forwards of All Time*. Minneapolis, MN: ABDO Publishing, 2015.
Readers discover the career highlights of the NBA's most famous forwards, including LeBron James.

Indovino, Shaina Carmel. *LeBron James*. Broomall, PA: Mason Crest, 2015.
This look into James's life traces his rise from at-risk youth to king of the NBA.

Lohre, Mike. *Six Degrees of LeBron James: Connecting Basketball Stars*. North Mankato, MN: Capstone Press, 2015.
Lohre reveals the connections between James and other basketball superstars, giving readers a deeper insight into the NBA.

Savage, Jeff. *LeBron James*. Minneapolis, MN: Lerner Publications, 2016.
Readers interested in learning more about James's life and career will find additional details in Savage's biography.

Taylor, Charlotte, and Stephen Feinstein. *LeBron James: Basketball Champion*. New York, NY: Enslow Publishing, 2016.
This book focuses on James's record-setting basketball career, including his multiple NBA championships.

Websites

Basketball Reference: LeBron James
(www.basketball-reference.com/players/j/jamesle01.html)
All of James's relevant statistics can be found on this website, along with statistics from players and teams throughout the history of the NBA.

The LeBron James Family Foundation
(lebronjamesfamilyfoundation.org/)
Discover the work being done by James's foundation, as well as ways you can help support its mission.

LeBron James: NBA Page (nba.com/playerfile/lebron_james)
James's player profile on the NBA's official website has important stats, videos, and a short biography.

LeBron James on Facebook (www.facebook.com/LeBron)
James's official Facebook page is where he shares photos, videos, and other posts to connect with his fans.

LeBron James on Instagram (www.instagram.com/kingjames)
Instagram allows James to post photos and allows his fans to like and comment on the glimpses into his life that he shares.

LeBron James on Twitter (twitter.com/KingJames)
James uses Twitter to interact with his fans through short messages of 140 characters or less.

The Official Website of LeBron James (lebronjames.com)
James's official website features links to information about different aspects of his life and career, including his charity work and business ventures.

Index

Picture Credits

Cover, p. 75 Jason Miller/Contributor/Getty Images Sport/ Getty Images; p. 7 Patrick Smith/Staff/Getty Images Sport/Getty Images; p. 10 Stephen Dunn/Staff/Getty Images Sport/Getty Images; p. 15 LUCY NICHOLSON/Stringer/AFP/Getty Images; p. 17 Steve Grayson/Contributor/WireImage/Getty Images; pp. 20, 23 Sporting News Archive/Contributor/Sporting News/ Getty Images; pp. 26, 29 REUTERS/Alamy Stock Photo; pp. 27, 85, 86 Ezra Shaw/Staff/Getty Images Sport/Getty Images; p. 30 Shareif Ziyadat/Contributor/FilmMagic/Getty Images; pp. 35, 71 Angelo Merendino/Contributor/Corbis Sport/Getty Images; p. 36 MCT/Contributor/Tribune News Service/Getty Images; p. 41 Larry Busacca/Staff/Getty Images Sport/Getty Images; p. 43 William Bryan/Contributor/Moment/Getty Images; p. 47 Greg Fiume/Stringer/Getty Images Sport/Getty Images; p. 49 Vallery Jean/Contributor/FilmMagic/Getty Images; p. 52 Miami Herald/Contributor/Tribune News Service/Getty Images; p. 53 Jared Wickerham/Stringer/Getty Images Sport/Getty Images; p. 55 epa european pressphoto agency/Alamy Stock Photo; p. 57 Mike Ehrmann/Staff/Getty Images Sport/Getty Images; p. 61 DON EMMERT/Staff/AFP/Getty Images; p. 64 Kevin C. Cox/Staff/Getty Images Sport/Getty Images; p. 67 Mark Wilson/Staff/Getty Images News/Getty Images; p. 69 Justin Sullivan/Staff/Getty Images News/Getty Images; p. 76 Michael Loccisano/Staff/Getty Images Entertainment/Getty Images; p. 80 FREDERIC J. BROWN/Staff/AFP/Getty Images.

About the Author

Ryan Nagelhout is an author and journalist who specializes in writing about sports. He has written hundreds of books, with topics ranging from baseball superstar David Ortiz, the Apollo 11 moon landing, and digital encryption and decryption. As a journalist he has covered sports, reviewed restaurants, and written features about the arts. Ryan has a bachelor's degree in Communication Studies from Canisius College in Buffalo, with a minor in Classics. He enjoys spending time with friends playing board games, bouldering, and hiking the Niagara Gorge in his hometown of Niagara Falls, New York.